TALES OF
A RUSSIAN GRANDMOTHER

By FRANCES CARPENTER

ILLUSTRATED BY I. BILIBINE

LORETO PUBLICATIONS
FITZWILLIAM NEW HAMPSHIRE
AD 2024

First Published: 1945
2024 Loreto Edition - All rights reserved
ISBN: 978-1-62292-402-8

Loreto Publications
P. O. Box 603
Fitzwilliam, NH 03447
603-239-6671— www.LoretoPubs.org

Editing: Jacob Sullivan
Layout and cover design by Michael Hamilton

Cover Image: Frontispiece from the book.

Printed and Bound in the United States of America

Nikita appeared and the princess gave him her gold ring.
Frontispiece

Contents

Contents

Illustrations

TALES OF
A RUSSIAN GRANDMOTHER

Nianya's
Little
Pigeons

OR several days the white snowflakes had been falling, falling. The great Russian country house had been hidden away from the outside world by swirling veils of white. From their playroom window, Kyril and his sister Sonia could not even see the tall birch tree at the corner of the house, so thick were the flying flakes.

Now at last the snow had ceased. The Russian countryside lay under a vast blanket of white. The branches of the trees were bent beneath their loads of clinging snow, and the outbuildings and peasants' huts about the great courtyard behind the house were almost smothered in white drifts.

"See, Kyril, the sun!" Sonia cried. "The sun has come out to light the way for our mother and father on their journey to St. Petersburg."

The boy ran to the window. He looked up at the gray sky and at the pale copper disk of the winter sun that was trying to force its way through the clouds.

"Yes, the snow has stopped for good," he said. "They will be able to go this afternoon surely."

Kyril and Sonia lived in Russia long ago, before the World War and the great Revolution that turned their land topsy-turvy and drove their family and friends from their comfortable homes. Their country was then governed by a powerful ruler whom they called the Tsar.

These two Russian children of those olden days dwelt far, far out in the country in a huge white house, at whose front door were round white columns much like those of the colonial homes in Virginia. Their father was rich. He owned countless acres of farms and forests, and thousands of peasants worked on his land. The children had never seen all of their father's estate. It would have taken them many days to ride on their ponies from one end of it to the other. When they went with their mother to make a call at the nearest country house, three galloping horses drew their sleigh swiftly over snowy roads for miles through the deep forests and across the broad plains. There was a village near by, to be sure, but in it there were only the white, green-domed church and one long street lined with the log huts of poor peasant farmers.

Each winter that they could remember, Kyril and Sonia had watched their father and mother start forth in their sleigh for the distant railroad station and for their yearly visit to the great city of St. Petersburg. On this day, as the hour for the departure drew near, the children ran to put on their long fur coats and their high felt boots. They pulled their fur caps over their ears and stood on the steps to see old Foka, the fat coachman, drive up the sleigh with its three splendid black horses, harnessed side by side, prancing and dancing over the snow.

"Hark, there are the bells!" Sonia exclaimed, even before the sleigh came into sight. The middle horse trotted under an arch of gilded wood that rose high above his shining black back; and upon this there hung little bells which tinkled gayly in the cold winter air. Kyril always admired the *troïka,* as this three-horse sleigh was called. He liked to see the red tassels dance and the brass trimmings of the harness sparkle as the horses tossed their fine heads and pawed up the snow.

"Old Foka looks just like a mushroom," the boy said to his sister. Sonia giggled, for the fat coachman in his flat hat and his padded black coat did remind her of the mushrooms that grew so thick in the meadows and under the trees in the autumn. Old Foka completely covered the tiny driver's seat of the sleigh. Icicles had already formed in his beard, and his cheeks were the color of very ripe cherries.

What a hubbub there always was at such a time as this! Servants rushing about with boxes and bundles! Mother and Father saying farewell to the children and their aunts, the governesses and the servants, and giving last orders to Nianya, the old nurse, who now had charge of the keys.

Sonia and Kyril enjoyed the excitement. They talked often together of the time when they should be old enough to go along with their parents to the magic city of St. Petersburg with its broad streets and its fine shops, its concerts and theatres, its dinners and dances.

Their mother kissed the rosy cheeks of her son and her daughter. Then she stepped lightly up into the sleigh. She pulled the collar of her fur coat high about her head and settled herself beside their father under the bearskin rugs. Old Foka took a firmer hold on the reins and braced his feet against the floor.

"God go with you, Little Father! God go with you, Mother dear!" Kyril and Sonia cried out, waving their mittened hands.

"God go with you, Master!" shouted the servants.

"Amen, God go with us!" the travelers replied, as Foka

cracked his whip and shouted to the horses. Away the sleigh dashed down the white roadway! Clouds of snow flew up from the horses' galloping feet. The bells tinkled wildly. Soon the sleigh was out of sight behind the birch trees. The sleigh bells could no longer be heard. The servants hurried indoors out of the biting cold. The great house and the vast land about it were still once again.

Kyril and Sonia stopped behind the others to throw handfuls of snow at each other. But Nianya, the old nurse, shook her head in its bright kerchief and called out to them.

"It is far too cold today, my little pigeons! You must come in at once. Your fingers will freeze."

Nianya could never remember that she was no longer in charge of Kyril and Sonia. She had been their nurse for so long, ever since they were wee babies. And indeed she had been nurse for their father before them. When Kyril and Sonia became old enough to have lessons, Nianya's rule ended. The peasant woman could neither read nor write, so of course she could not teach the children the things they must know. Then their days were divided up between their French "Mademoiselle," their English "Miss," and the German tutor, who had charge of the schooling of the older boys and girls of the family.

But Nianya still felt responsible for her "little pigeons,"

her *"golub-chicki"* as she often called them. Even in the midst of her many new duties—for Nianya was now housekeeper of the great house—she always had time to keep an eye on the children, and to spoil them, the strict English governess declared.

The Russian boy and his sister were not lonely during the months their parents spent in gay St. Petersburg. So many people lived in their house with them and in the peasants' cottages out on the courtyard. There was Aunt Olga, who was in charge of the establishment during their mother's absence. There was Aunt Varvara, who directed the peasant girls in the spinning and weaving room. There was Cousin Elena, who ruled in the dairy and the poultry houses; and old Uncle Feodor, who spent much of his time with the men who wove baskets and worked in the carpenter shop. And then there were all the servants who kept the big house in order, who cooked in the kitchens, who served in the dining rooms, and who cared for the huge porcelain stoves that warmed the high-ceilinged rooms.

Nianya directed the linen rooms and the great storerooms between the brick arches in the cellar under the house. Kyril and Sonia liked to go down there with her when she got out the supplies for the day.

Every nook and corner of the cellar was stored with some kind of food. In a bed of dry sand in the center there were buried the turnips, the carrots, the parsnips, and the potatoes. Huge casks set in rows held salt beef and salt fish, and the pickled cabbages and beets from which the daily soups were made. Smoked mutton, smoked hams, sides of bacon, and strings of dried mushrooms hung from the low ceiling.

The keys that unlocked the heavy padlocks on the storeroom doors were kept on a chain fastened to Nianya's belt. She weighed out each pound of flour, sugar, and rice. She counted each bag of salt and each golden cheese. It took a great deal of food to feed the fifty mouths of this country household. But yet, Nianya thought, there was no need to waste, and besides, the supplies had to last through the six long winter months.

Winters are cold in the land where Kyril and Sonia lived. And cold weather means big appetites. In the home of a poor peasant, the hungry children had to fill their stomachs from the great bowl of cabbage soup, set out for each meal on their rude table, and with chunks of black bread made from the rye grown by their father. But in a rich country house, like that of Kyril and Sonia, the fare was far better.

"Until I came here to live," Nianya often said to the two children, "I had never seen bread so white, nor such good cabbage soup with bits of meat and sausage swimming about in it. At first I ate and I ate until I almost made myself sick."

Kyril and Sonia liked to put thick sour cream into their good cabbage soup, for they thought this gave it a far better taste. They were especially fond of *blini*, those golden brown pancakes over which they poured hot melted butter. Their porridge, which they called *kasha*, was made of finely ground buckwheat. They ate also a good deal of fish that had been caught in the river Volga which flowed through their land.

Nianya always kept a few dried sunflower seeds in the pocket of her apron for her "little pigeons." The Russian children liked to chew these, just as the children of other lands like to nibble nuts.

On this winter afternoon, when Kyril and Sonia had shaken the snow from their high felt out-of-door boots, they came into the wide entrance hall of their home. Nianya helped to take off their fur coats and caps, and she drew up two chairs beside the tall porcelain stove so that they might sit and warm their numbed fingers and toes against its pretty blue tiles.

The bright-eyed, rosy-cheeked peasant woman looked down fondly at the two children. She dearly loved this yellow-haired boy and his sister, with their blue eyes and fine fair skin. Kyril was even then wearing a Russian blouse which she had embroidered for him. It was of soft white linen, and its gay border was finely cross-stitched in a bright red and black pattern. The boy wore his blouse outside his dark-colored trousers, and a belt of soft leather held it close to his waist. His legs were covered with boots that reached to his knees.

Sonia was dressed just like a little French girl. Her frock had come from a French shop in St. Petersburg, and her golden hair was tied back with a broad silken ribbon. Nianya always thought her "little pigeons" the prettiest children in the whole world. Indeed, the Russians are a handsome people. They are tall and broad-shouldered, and the faces of the nobles of the olden days were often fine and intelligent.

Nianya herself was pleasant to look upon. Her wrinkled cheeks were rosy, and her blue eyes were bright. Her striped apron was always clean, and the kerchief she wore tied over her head was of gay colored cotton.

"Tell us of the time before you came to live here, Nianya dear," Kyril asked, as they warmed themselves at the stove.

"And of how your father asked our grandfather to take you into his service," Sonia added quickly.

"*Ai, ai,* my little pigeons!" the peasant woman said kindly. "Why talk of my poor home here in the midst of these beautiful rooms with their soft rugs and fine paintings and their other rich treasures? The little hut where I was born could be set down in your parlor and not touch walls or ceiling. It was just like all the other huts of all the other peasants down there in the village. Between its log walls and under its roof of straw thatch there were but two rooms. We stored the farm tools and the grain in one. We lived in the other.

"And how many there were of us! I was the lucky one, for I was the youngest, and my father and mother always took me to sleep with them on the broad shelf that was built out over the stove. It was good and warm there on a winter night, I can tell you. My brothers and sisters slept on the wood benches which they pulled up as near to the stove as they could. We never took off our clothes save on Saturday night, when we went to the village steam bath to make ourselves clean for church Sunday morning.

"But if you only think of it, what a big world God's world is! In it there are rich folk and poor folk as well. And there is room for them all. We were happy, too," Nianya said, nodding her head. "In the long winter evenings my father would tell us stories, and such stories they were! About wood nymphs and water sprites, hobgoblins and fairies. All the tales I tell you I learned from him. It was through his story-telling that I came to live here. *Da!** It happened this way.

"One day the master summoned my father to the great house to entertain his hunting guests with songs and tales of the old witch, Baba-Yaga, and the other fairy folk. That was the beginning. The end was that your grandfather gave me a place here in the great house to help the head nurse care for your father and his brothers and sisters. And here I have been ever since, except for the time when I lived with my poor husband in our cottage out on the courtyard."

Nianya had been for nearly fifty years on this estate. Even when her children were little, she helped in the great

*Yes.

house. One of her daughters married Vanya, the estate blacksmith who cared for the feet of the horses and repaired the farm tools. Her little grandchildren often played with Kyril and Sonia on the snowy hillsides beyond the courtyard.

"You are our real grandmother, Nianya dear," Sonia would sometimes whisper to the old woman as she was tucking her into bed. "We like you better than our father's mother who lives in St. Petersburg so far away. When she comes to visit us here, she seems like a stranger. She does not tell us fairy tales as you do."

Indeed, Nianya was fonder of Kyril and Sonia than of her own grandchildren. She had cared for them for so long that they seemed like her own. The children spent many happy hours sitting beside her as she mended the household linen or made her fine cross-stitch embroidery. Each chance they got, they would run out from the schoolroom, or they would slip away while the older people drank their tall glasses of hot tea about the copper samovar each morning and afternoon. They would seek out their beloved Nianya and beg for a *skazka,* one of the famous old Russian fairy tales that are now so well known far and wide over the world.

Nianya was a good woman. She went regularly to the white church with the green domes and gold crosses in the village near by. Each day she said her prayers before the holy picture which she called her "icon" and which stood on a shelf in the corner of her room. She believed every word the village priest said about God and His saints. But she half believed also in the fairies of which she told Kyril and Sonia. She was sure there were fairy people in the forests and on the plains, in the lakes and the rivers, and even in the very pool in the garden of the great house. She had heard the *skazki* from her father. He had them from his father, and so they must be true.

The Frost King's Bride

"I HAVE mending to do," Nianya said, turning away from the porcelain stove in the wide entrance hall.

"We shall come with you, Nianya, and you shall tell us a *skazka*," Kyril cried, jumping up from his chair.

"Please, dear little Nianya," Sonia begged pleadingly. "Mademoiselle is boiling the hot water in the samover for the afternoon tea. They will not miss us for a good while."

The children followed old Nianya up to the linen room on the second floor of the great house. The woman got out her mending basket and settled her spectacles on her broad nose. She drew her chair up to the window so that she could see better. Then she looked up at the boy and the girl, waiting so eagerly for the fairy tale which they were sure was to come.

"Well, today is a good day for the tale of the red-nosed Frost King and his gentle bride. Look at that third pine tree yonder, so covered with snow. There's Morosko, the red-nosed Frost King himself!"

Kyril and Sonia followed the direction of her pointing finger. Through the double windows of thick glass they gazed at the tall pine tree. The snow clung to it in great tufts, and it did indeed look like a man. The thick clump on its tip top was shaped like the black sheepskin cap that Kyril had just taken off. Two spreading branches, coated with snow, were stretched out like long arms and waved in the breeze.

"*Da!* It was a day just like this when poor Marfa went forth to find her icy bridegroom. But I must begin back at the beginning.

"Once long ago, there was an old man who had three daughters. The eldest was the gentle Marfa, whose mother was dead. The other two were Masha and Vera, the children of the old man's second wife, who now ruled his house.

"Poor Marfa had a hard lot. From morning till night her stepmother and her stepsisters scolded and grumbled.

16

Marfa's work was the hardest. She had to rise before it was light to fetch the wood and the water. She had to make the fires in the stoves and give food to the animals. All day long she toiled, but still her stepmother was cross.

" 'What a lazy-bones you are!' she would grumble at Marfa. 'What an untidy creature! The pots and pans are not in their places. The oven fork does not stand straight in its corner. Our hut is full of dust and dirt!'

"The poor girl would say nothing. She would wipe away her tears on the edge of her apron and do all that she could to please her stepmother and her stepsisters. The sisters were just as bad as their mother. Cross, and scolding her all the time! Quarreling and making poor Marfa cry! They themselves lay late on the ledge over the stove and washed themselves with the water that Marfa had brought. They sat down to their work only when they had filled their stomachs with good hot soup. So the three girls grew up, and at last the time came when they were ready to marry.

"A tale is soon told, my little pigeons, but not so quickly do things happen. The old man loved Marfa because she was so gentle and good. He was sorry for her, but he did not know how to help her. He was old, he was sick; and he was afraid of his wife.

"Well, the father thought and thought how to get husbands for his three daughters. The stepmother thought, too, but her thought was chiefly how to rid herself of the stepdaughter she hated. One evening after supper she said to her husband, 'Well, old man, let us first find a husband for Marfuska.'*

" 'All right,' said the old man, as he climbed wearily up on his bed over the stove.

" 'Tomorrow morning, rise early,' the woman ordered him. 'Harness the horse and get the sledge ready! And you, Marfuska, pack your things into a box. You shall go with your father to visit your bridegroom.'

"Good Marfa was pleased that she was to go visiting. All through the night she slept soundly and sweetly. Early next morning she washed herself and combed her hair. She read her prayers before the holy icon and then packed her things into a box. She dressed herself in her best, and a fine sight she was, too. Never a better bride could you wish to see. Before dawn the old man had the sledge at the door. He entered the hut and sat down on a bench.

" 'Are you ready, Little Marfa?' he said to his daughter.

" 'I'm ready, Father dear.'

" 'Well, if you are ready,' the stepmother cried, 'sit down and eat quickly.' She gave them a hunk of black bread and a few swallows of cabbage soup. 'Eat quickly

*Little Marfa.

and begone! I've seen enough of you! Old man, drive away as fast as you can! Be sure you go as I say! Drive along the road to the forest, then turn to the right. In the deep dark woods there, you will find a tall pine tree. Leave Marfuska under it. Her bridegroom will come for her, the fine young gallant, Morosko the Frost King.'

"The old man opened his eyes very wide. He left off eating his soup. Poor Marfa began to weep and to moan.

" 'How now!' cried the woman. 'Stop all that noise! Why should you weep? Your bridegroom is handsome. And very rich, too! Just look at his wealth! All the pines and the firs and the birches covered with silver! PeoPle will surely envy you being the bride of such a great King.'

"The old man was afraid for poor Marfa. But he did not dare disobey his ill-tempered wife. I don't know whether their journey was short or long. But the old man followed directions. He put the girl down under the tall pine tree in the midst of the dark forest. Then he turned his horses round and drove the sledge off home again.

"Marfa sat on her trunk and trembled all over, it was so cold. She could scarcely breathe. She wanted to cry, but no tears would come. Suddenly she heard a noise. The pine trees crackled. She knew at once that it was Morosko the Frost King, jumping from one tree to another. She could hear his fingers snap and she could feel his icy breath. At last the Frost King spoke to the girl from the top of the very pine tree beneath which she was sitting.

" 'Are you warm, Maiden? Are you quite warm, Pretty One?'

" 'Oh, quite warm, dear King Frost,' Marfa replied gently, through her chattering teeth.

"The Frost King climbed down nearer, snapping his icy fingers louder and louder.

" 'Are you warm, Maiden?' he asked. 'Are you quite warm?'

" 'Oh, yes, dear Frost, I am quite, quite warm.'

"The red-nosed Frost King crackled still louder.

" 'Are you warm, Maiden? Are you warm, my pretty dove?' he asked for a third time. The girl was beginning to freeze. Her lips were so stiff that she could scarce answer.

" 'Oh, my dear, dear Frost, warmth comes from God and cold comes from God!' she whispered faintly. Then the Frost King took pity upon the gentle maiden. He wrapped her in a fine fur cloak, and he warmed her in blankets.

"Next morning the woman sent her old husband out with the sledge to find her stepdaughter. In the meantime she began to bake cakes for the girl's funeral. Then the little dog, lying under the table, suddenly spoke:

" 'Taff! Taff!' he barked.

" *'The master's daughter comes in silver and gold,*
  But the mistress's daughters will die in the cold.'

" 'Be still, you booby!' cried the woman. 'Here is a pancake! Now say instead:

" ' *"The master's daughter is still with cold,*
  But the mistress's daughters shall have silver and gold." '

"The little dog swallowed the pancake whole, but he spoke again as before:

" *'The master's daughter comes in silver and gold,*
  But the mistress's daughters will die in the cold.'

"And he kept on saying this until the woman drove him out of the house.

"Well, wasn't the woman angry and surprised when she saw the old man bringing Marfa home, safe and sound, wrapped in a fine fur cloak and with her trunk full of linen and gold and silver gifts from the Frost King!

"Are you warm, maiden?" the frost king asked.

" 'Do not unhitch the sledge!' she ordered the old man. 'Turn the horses round! You shall drive my daughters also to the Frost King and he will give them far richer gifts even than these.'

"The old man brought the two grumbling girls to the very same pine tree, and he set them down there with their belongings. Then he drove away. The two girls laughed to each other.

" 'What an odd idea of our mother's it was to bring us here for a bridegroom! Are there not enough boys to marry in our own village? Who knows but that the devil himself may not come here! Then what should we do?'

"The girls were dressed in thick sheepskin coats. Yet they began to shiver and shake. 'Listen to me, sister,' said Masha. 'The frost is chilling my bones. What if only one bridegroom comes? Which will he choose?'

" 'I suppose you think that it will be you,' her sister cried angrily.

" 'Well, are you so sure that it will be yourself?' Masha said sharply.

"And so they set to quarreling. Just then the Frost King began to snap his fingers and to jump from pine tree to pine tree. The girls heard the tinkling noise in the icy branches and thought their bridegroom was coming.

" 'Hark, Masha, he comes!' said Vera, shivering. 'He drives with bells on his sledge.'

"Nearer and nearer came the Frost King. At last he was in the very top of the tall pine tree under which the girls were sitting.

" 'Are you warm, Maidens?' he asked. 'Are you warm, Little Pigeons?'

" 'No, we are nearly frozen to death,' the girls replied crossly. 'We are waiting for our bridegroom, but he has gone and lost himself, drat him!' Lower and lower climbed the red-nosed Frost King. Louder and louder was the snapping and crackling.

" 'Are you warm, Maidens? Are you warm, Pretty Ones?'

" 'Go away, do not bother us!' was the rude answer. 'Can't you see we are frozen?'

"Still lower and lower bent the Frost King. Louder and louder he snapped his icy fingers; and harder and harder he breathed on the two maidens. Soon they were quite stiff.

"Next morning the woman sent her old man out to fetch back her daughters.

" 'Take warm blankets with you,' she cried. 'And be sure to leave room for their trunks and their treasures. They will surely bring back baskets of linen and gifts of silver and gold.'

"Quickly the old man drove out to the pine tree in the dark forest. The woman was just finishing her breakfast when the little dog under the table began to bark once again:

"'Taff! Taff!

"'*The master's daughter came with silver and gold,*
But the mistress's daughters are stiff with cold.'

"'Do not tell such lies,' the old woman screamed to the dog. 'Here is a hot cake for you. Say the verse so:

"''*The mistress's daughters come with silver and gold,*
While the master's daughter will be stiff with cold.''

"But the little dog would not. He barked again:
"'Taff! Taff!

"'*The master's daughter came with silver and gold,*
But the mistress's daughters——'

"The woman would not let the dog finish. She was just driving him out of the hut when she saw the sledge coming home. When she looked under the blanket and found her two daughters lying frozen and stiff, she flew into a rage.

"'What have you done with my little dears?' she screamed at her husband.

" 'Keep still, woman,' he cried. 'You were too greedy for riches, and your daughters were too ill-tempered! It is all your own fault. You would have it so!'

"Well, the woman scolded and raged. But afterwards she made peace with her husband and Marfa. They went on living and thriving and forgetting the past. Soon a good boy from the village came to woo Marfa. They had a fine wedding feast, and the old man used to frighten his grandchildren with this tale of Morosko, the red-nosed Frost King. He did not let them have their way, as I let you have yours."

Sadko the Rich Merchant

IT WAS on the evening of the sixth day of January. Nianya had come into Sonia's room just before bedtime, and the two children were telling her of their journey to the river Volga to see the great "Blessing of the Waters." This festival took place each Twelfth-tide all over old Russia, but this was the first time that Kyril and Sonia had gone along with the others to see it for themselves.

"Oh, Nianya, dear, it was splendid!" Sonia cried eagerly. "We started so early and our *troïka* fairly flew along over the snow. We were among the first to arrive."

"You should have seen the huge ice cross they had set up on the river," Kyril broke in. "It glittered like diamonds. And the procession was grand, with the priests and the village fathers carrying the holy icons and banners. All the peasants from our town and the next were there."

"They sang so loud and clear, Nianya," Sonia took up the story again. "It was as if all God's world were a huge church. Our own Vanya from the blacksmith shop was one of the men chosen to chop a hole in the thick ice of the river. And how still everyone was! We all stood about the ice cross in a great circle while the priest read the services. Aunt Varvara says that the waters of Russia are blessed so every year because Christ blessed the Jordan when He was baptized."

"That's true, my treasure," the peasant woman said, nodding her head in its bright cotton kerchief, "and a good thing it is, too, that our waters are blessed and the naughty fairies and sprites sent down under the ice. You know, my little pigeons, in winter time our air is filled with all the spirits and the hobgoblins who can no longer play in their pools and their ponds. With his ice and his snow, King Frost has shut them out of their homes. Where should they go but into our houses? They fly about through our woods and over our fields.

"As the holy procession marches down the river, the fairies hear the sweet chanting. They follow and join it. You cannot see them, perhaps, but they are there just the same. When the priest blesses the waters and sprinkles the holy drops all about, the fairies lose their magic power. They are forced to jump into that hole cut in the river. The hole freezes over again before the priest finishes his chanting. So the naughty fairies are shut up under the ice sure and safe until the spring thaw comes once again."

"But Mademoiselle says there are no fairies at all," Kyril objected.

"*Och*, some people do say that," the old woman cried, shaking her head in dismay. "But they will find out, like Sadko the Rich Merchant."

"Who was Sadko?" Sonia cried.

"Oh, tell us about him, Nianya," begged Kyril.

"Well, I will tell you, and then you shall see what happens when people pay no attention to the folk that live under the water!" Nianya exclaimed.

"Once long ago, upon the great Caspian Sea, there sailed thirty ships. Fine ships they were. And filled with rich goods. Like splendid falcons, they sped about over the waters. And the finest and swiftest was the ship of Sadko the Rich Merchant. For twelve long years Sadko had sailed the rivers and seas. And with each year of the twelve, he had grown richer and richer with his trade on the waters.

"One day when Sadko the Rich Merchant sailed at the

head of the thirty falcon ships, his vessel suddenly stopped. No wind filled his sails. His ship lay still on the water. But the other ships passed swiftly. Their sails were swelled by strong breezes. Sadko's seamen cried out with wonder. They could not understand why their ship should stand still while the others went on. Then Sadko spoke:

" 'O ye seamen and ye serving men! I, Sadko, know why we are becalmed. Twelve years have I sailed these waters so blue. Yet not once have I paid tribute to the Tsar who dwells under the sea. Not one grain of corn nor one pinch of salt have I thrown into his waters. Now he is angry. One of us must be sent to him to calm his great wrath.

" 'Which one shall it be?' asked Sadko the Rich Merchant. 'Let us each throw a chip of wood into the blue water. Those whose chips shall float high upon the blue waves shall remain on the ship. But whose chip shall sink deep, he shall drown and go to the Tsar of the Sea!'

"It was done. The chips were all named and cast over the side of the ship. And all the chips floated. Like the ducks in our pond, they swam on the waters. That is, all but one. And that one was the chip of Sadko, himself.

" '*Tfu!*' Sadko cried. 'It is not right that I, Sadko, should drown. Let us try once again. Let us once more throw our chips into the blue sea. Let each write his name on a fresh willow chip. And this time let it be that those whose ships shall sink deep shall remain on the ship. That one whose chip floats high on the blue waves, he shall drown and be sent to the Tsar of the Sea.'

"So it was done. To be sure that this time his cast should sink deep, Sadko the Rich Merchant wrote his name upon a blade of hard shining steel. And the weight of the steel blade was heavy—oh, heavy! Into the blue waves Sadko threw the steel blade. But, wonder of wonders, the willow chips fell deep, deep to the sea bottom. And the great steel blade of Sadko rose to the top and floated high on the blue waves.

" 'Och, there is no other way,' sighed Sadko the Rich Merchant. 'The Sea Tsar will have none other than me. I must go to my death. O ye seaman and ye serving men, bring me my fur cloak. I go to my drowning. I go to pay homage to the Tsar of the Sea.'

"Sadko was soon ready. He did not forget to take along with him his harp with the fine golden strings. He did not leave behind his great chessboard with its figures of gold. A silver-gilt boat was launched from the ship, and in this he started forth on his sad journey.

"At once Sadko's own ship rode again on the waves like a splendid falcon. And all the thirty ships sailed away on the sea like so many swift birds. Only Sadko was left alone on the tossing blue waters.

"Great is the power of our parents' prayers, my little pigeons," Nianya continued her tale, nodding her head. "And great was the power of the prayers of Sadko's parents. Surely they must have prayed long before their holy icons that day. For a calm came on the waves and breezes blew gently. Sadko the Rich Merchant was carried safely and swiftly along in his silver-gilt boat. On and on over the blue waters he went! He saw neither hills nor shore, but all at once he was swept up on a broad beach. Before him there stood a great palace of gold, and in it he found the Tsar of the Sea, taking his ease.

" 'Hail, O Sadko Rich Merchant Man,' the Tsar exclaimed. 'Now at last has God granted me my desire. Twelve years have I waited for a visit from Sadko, to whom I have given such wealth and such treasure. Now Sadko has come to me of his own free will to play chess with me and to make me sweet music on his golden-stringed harp. Play for me now, O Sadko.'

"So Sadko began to amuse the Tsar of the Sea. He struck up a tune on his sweet-singing harp. The Sea Tsar rose from his seat and began to dance. He danced and he danced. He gave rich drinks to Sadko and bade him play on. He danced and he danced. And again he gave drinks to Sadko the Rich Merchant Man. At last Sadko fell into

In his dream there came to him our good saint Nicholas
saying, "O Sadko, beware!"

a sound sleep. But the golden strings of the harp still gave forth their sweet music.

"Soundly Sadko slept. And in his dream there came to him our good Saint Nicholas, saying, 'O Sadko, beware! Tear out those golden strings and fling them away! For the Tsar of the Waters has danced far too much. The blue sea above has been roaring and tossing and rolling and tumbling. The rivers have flowed out over the land. Ships are being wrecked. Sailors are drowning. Play no more, Sadko, upon thy sweet-singing harp.'

"Up jumped the rich Sadko. He tore the golden strings out of his harp and he threw them away. The Sea Tsar stopped dancing. Straightway the waves of the sea became calm, and the rivers flowed back into their beds.

" 'Mend your harp, O Sadko,' the Sea Tsar cried out. 'Mend your harp so that I may dance on and on!' But Sadko replied that he could not mend his harp. 'Only in my own Novgorod town can my harp be mended, O Tsar of the Sea,' Sadko declared.

" 'Well, go, then, O Sadko,' the Sea Tsar said sadly. 'But before you depart, you shall take a bride. Thirty daughters I have. Tomorrow I will bring them before you and you shall choose for yourself the one who pleases you most.'

"That night the Tsar of the Sea again gave Sadko rich

drinks until he fell into a deep slumber. And again there came to him in his dream our good Saint Nicholas.

" 'Sadko,' said the Saint, 'heed what I tell thee. When the Tsar of the Sea brings the thirty maidens before thee, do not choose the fairest. Choose instead the one who is the least lovely.'

"When Sadko awoke, he did as the good saint had bidden him. He chose the least fair of all the daughters of the Tsar of the Sea. And lo, with her he received a great treasure of gold and silver, of jewels and gems. For the one he had chosen was the Sea Tsar's favorite, and of all the thirty maidens, her dowry was greatest.

"That night when Sadko laid himself down to rest, he dreamed that he was back again in his Novgorod town. It seemed as if he were standing on the banks of his own river Volkov. He saw his own house. He saw the great church of Nicolai Mojaisk. And he saw all his family running forward to meet him.

"When he awoke he found his dream had come true. He was indeed once again on the banks of his own river and beside him were all the silver and gold, the jewels and gems that the Tsar of the Sea had given to him. Only his mermaid bride was no longer beside him.

"Thereafter thirty ships sped over the waters. Like falcons they flew. And at the head of them all sailed the ship of Sadko the Rich Merchant. Not a year passed without some gift for the Tsar of the Sea from Sadko and his sailors. And not a year passed without Sadko's ships bringing great wealth into the custom house. Rich indeed now was Sadko the Merchant. Worth thousands and thousands and thousands he was. So great was his wealth that it took him three days to look through it all."

The Little Sister of the Sun

YRIL and Sonia had been coasting with Nianya's grandson, Nicolai, whom they called Kolya for short. Wrapped in their fur coats, with their fur caps pulled well over their ears and their feet snug in high felt snow boots, they did not feel the crisp cold of the icy winter air. Their peasant playmate was warm in coat and cap of thick sheepskin. Again and again the children had slid down the slopes of the snow-covered fields, laughing and shouting at the tops of their voices.

The land all about them was a shining world of white. Under the bright sun the ice-covered trees glittered and sparkled. The snowy blanket that covered the earth stretched as far as they could see, like a vast white desert.

The mid-winter sun dropped nearer and nearer the edge of the forests off to the west. It became colder and colder.

"We shall have to go in," Kyril said to Kolya at last. "The days are so short now. The sun will soon be gone."

"Let's go and find Nianya," Sonia cried to her brother as they trudged over the snow, back to the house. "She will give us some cake. I'm hungry as a wolf."

Sonia and Kyril had changed their wet clothing and were standing at the window of Kyril's room when Nianya appeared. The woman carried a tray on which there were sun play over the snow. Each white bush and each tall plate heaped high with crisp gingerbread cookies.

"Look at the sun, Nianya dear," Sonia cried out to her old nurse. "See how it paints pictures on the white snow!"

The children were watching the rosy rays of the setting sun play over the snow. Each white bush and each tall white-coated tree was bathed in bright rose color. Green shadows fell across the glittering lawn in front of the house. As they watched, the sky changed to orange and the shadows darkened to blue.

"What beautiful colors!" Sonia exclaimed.

"Yes, my dove," Nianya said, "the Little Sister of the Sun is using her paint brush."

"The Little Sister of the Sun? Who is she, Nianya?" Kyril asked quickly. "Is there a story about her?"

"Why, surely you know that the sun has a sister," said old Nianya, turning to arrange the tea things on the table. "Have I never told you the tale of the Tsar's son who went to live with the Sun's sister in her beautiful palace high up in the sky? Well, eat your ginger cakes and drink your tea while it is hot, and I'll tell it to you now!"

While Kyril and Sonia sipped their pale golden tea through lumps of sugar held between their white teeth, old Nianya told them this tale of Sergei and the Little Sister of the Sun.

"In a certain kingdom in a far distant state, there once lived a Tsar and his wife, the Tsarina," Nianya began. "They had only one son, a boy called Sergei, who, alas, had been dumb from the day of his birth. Not a word did he speak, although he could hear as well as you or I.

"But Sergei Son-of-the-Tsar was a good child. All in the great palace loved him dearly. The boy used to go every day down to the stables, and of the stablemen there was one whom he liked above all the others. This groom used to tell him fairy tales such as I tell you, my little pigeons.

"One day when Sergei Son-of-the-Tsar was about twelve years old, he went down as usual to find his friend, the stableman. But this day it was no fairy story he heard. *Och*, it was quite another sort of a tale.

" 'Sergei Son-of-the-Tsar,' the groom said to the lad,

'listen to me. Soon there will be born to your mother, the Tsarina, a daughter, your sister. But when she grows up she will turn into a witch. She will eat your mother and father and you, too, if she can. You must go away. Ask your father, the Tsar, for the very best steed in his royal stables. Speak calmly as if you wanted to go for a ride! Then fly far, far away and do not come back.'

"The boy ran to his father. He opened his mouth and, for the first time in his life, words came from his lips. The Tsar was so glad at the wonderful happening that he did not even ask his son why he wanted the horse. He straightway gave orders that the very best in all the stables should be saddled for Sergei.

"Sergei Son-of-the-Tsar rode away and away, to where his eyes led him. On and on he rode for a long time. Then he grew weary of riding, and he came to a hut where two old women sat sewing.

" 'Little Mothers,' said Sergei, 'take me to dwell with you.'

" 'Gladly, Sergei Son-of-the-Tsar,' the women replied. 'But alas we ourselves have not long to live. As soon as we have broken the last of these needles, and as soon as we have used up the last of the thread in this chest here beside us, then we shall die.'

"Sergei Son-of-the-Tsar wept with the two women. He

was sorry for the old creatures, and he rode away sadly. Long, long he rode. At last he came to a forest where he found a man tearing oak trees out of the ground by their roots.

" 'Take me to dwell with you, O Man-Who-Tears-Up-Oak-Trees,' he begged the woodsman.

" 'Gladly would I take you, Sergei Son-of-the-Tsar,' the woodsman replied. 'But alas, I myself have not long to live in God's good world. As soon as I have uprooted the last of these oak trees, then I shall die.'

"Still more bitterly did the kind-hearted Sergei weep as he went on his way. He rode on and on for a long time—oh, a long time. At last he met a man who was busy turning over the mountains.

" 'Take me to dwell with you, O Man-Who-Turns-Over-Mountains,' said Sergei Son-of-the-Tsar.

" 'Gladly,' was the reply. 'But alas, I myself have not long to live. As soon as I have turned over the last of these mountains, then my death will come.'

"Sergei Son-of-the-Tsar shed more bitter tears at the thought of the sad fate of the Man-Who-Turns-Over-Mountains. He rode on for a long time, and at last he came to the great palace of the Little Sister of the Sun. She took him in gladly and gave him food and drink. She

tended the lad as if he were her brother. And long did he
dwell with her. His life should indeed have been easy and
happy. But Sergei grew homesick. He longed to know what
had happened back in his own country. One day he
climbed up a high mountain and looked down into the
palace.

" 'Alas, the stableman's story was true,' he cried aloud as
he gazed. 'The wicked witch has eaten up my mother and
father. Only the walls of the empty palace remain.' And
he wept loud and long.

" 'Why are your eyes so red, Sergei Son-of-the-Tsar?'

asked the Little Sister of the Sun, when the young man returned.

" 'The wind has made my eyes red,' Sergei replied. So the Little Sister of the Sun ordered the wind to stop blowing. But Sergei could not help weeping when he thought of his dear father and mother. So he had to confess why his eyes were so red. He begged the Sun's Sister to allow him to return to his own country. At first she would not. But he begged and he begged. And at last she gave in.

" 'Take these gifts with you, O Sergei Son-of-the-Tsar. They will be of use,' said the Sun's Little Sister, putting into his hand a brush and a comb and two ripe red apples.

"On his way home, Sergei Son-of-the-Tsar met the Man-Who-Turns-Over-Mountains. Only one mountain now was left standing, and the Man-Who-Turns-Over-Mountains was almost ready to die. Something told Sergei to throw down his brush upon the open field. He did so, and suddenly there sprang up out of the ground many tall mountains whose peaks reached the sky. One there was for each bristle of his magic brush. There were so many that you could never have counted them all. The Man-Who-Turns-Over-Mountains set to work again gladly, rejoiced that he might yet live for a while.

"Sergei rode on again. I do not know whether he rode for a long time or for a short time, but at last he came up to the Man-Who-Tears-Up-Oak-Trees. Only three trees were left standing, and the poor man was making ready to die. Something told Sergei to throw down his comb upon the open field, and straightway there sprang up from the earth a dense forest of oak trees. The Man-Who-Tears-Up-Oak-Trees was overjoyed at the thought of living a while longer. He gave thanks to the Tsar's son and went about his business of tearing the great forest trees out of the ground.

"Sergei then rode on. At last he came to the two old women for whom he had felt so sorry and sad. He gave to each one a ripe red apple, and as soon as they had eaten them, they were transformed into lovely young maidens again. The women were so happy that they made Sergei a present of a magic kerchief. One had but to wave it from one side to the other and a lake would spread out behind him, so they told the young prince.

"At home once again in the Tsar's palace, Sergei Son-of-the-Tsar was met by his witch-sister, who greeted him tenderly. She spoke soft words to him, saying:

" 'Sit down, brother dear, and play on this guitar. I will go and make dinner ready.' The Tsar's son was sitting, playing upon the guitar, when a little mouse crept out of its hole in the floor. It spoke to him thus:

" 'Save yourself, Sergei Son-of-the-Tsar! Run away quickly! Your sister, the witch, has gone to sharpen her teeth.'

"Sergei dashed out of the palace and mounted his steed. He rode away at a gallop. The kind little mouse ran up and down on the strings of his guitar, so that the witch-sister might think that the prince was still playing. At last, when she had sharpened her teeth, the witch rushed in, meaning to devour Sergei. The tip of the mouse's tail was just disappearing into the hole when she entered the room. How angry she was! She gnashed her sharp teeth and rushed out of the palace after her brother.

"When he saw the witch coming, the youth waved his magic handkerchief from one side to the other. A deep lake spread out behind him. But the witch swam across it and came on even faster. The Man-Who-Tears-Up-Oak-Trees saw that Sergei was now in great trouble. So he began pulling up one tree after another and throwing them into a heap on the highroad. A whole mountain of oaks he threw in the path of the wicked witch-sister.

"With her sharp teeth the witch began to gnaw her way through them. She gnawed and she gnawed. At last she got through and rushed after Sergei. She was about to catch up with him when the Man-Who-Turns-Over-Mountains upset the highest peak of them all, right in her way. It took the witch some time to climb up the steep cliffs, but at last she succeeded. After Sergei she rushed, and she was just overtaking him when the youth galloped up to the palace of the Little Sister of the Sun.

" 'Open the window! Open! Open!' Sergei cried in distress.

"The Sun's Sister threw the window wide open, and Sergei Son-of-the-Tsar jumped through, horse and all. His witch-sister hammered upon the door of the house. She demanded that the Sun's Sister should give her brother up to her. But the Little Sister of the Sun steadfastly refused.

" 'Well, then, let the balance decide it,' the crafty witch said. 'Let Sergei stand on one side and I shall stand on the other. We shall know which of us is the greater. He who weighs less shall be the loser.' The Little Sister of the Sun smiled to herself, for she had thought of a plan to outwit the witch.

"The brother and sister went to the scales—and huge ones they were, my dears, like those out in our barn on which the men weigh sacks of grain. Sergei Son-of-the-Tsar climbed first into one side of the great balance. Then the witch scrambled up. As soon as she stepped on her side of the balance, up the other side flew; and Sergei Son-of-the-Tsar was thrown high into the air. So high did he fly that he went right into the open window of the palace of the Little Sister of the Sun. And he never came out again. His wicked witch-sister was forced to turn herself round and go back to the earth."

The Chudo Yudo with Twelve Heads

"OUR days are too short, Nianya," said Kyril one winter evening. "We have light for such a few hours, and the dark comes so soon."

In the northern land where Kyril and Sonia lived, the sun shows its face for only four hours each day in the mid-winter season. The time for play out-of-doors for this boy and girl always seemed far too short. They often complained to their old nurse when the dark had driven them in from their coasting or skiing or their games out in the snow.

"You must not complain, my little falcon," said the old woman. "Now if you had lived in the days of Ivan Pop-yaloff, you might have had reason. For then there was no daylight at all. All over his land it was always night."

"How could that be, Nianyuska?"* Sonia cried wondering.

"It was the doing of the Chudo Yudos," Nianya replied.

"What were the Chudo Yudos?" Kyril asked.

"If you will not interrupt, I will explain," said the old woman. She settled herself more comfortably in her low chair and took up her knitting.

"The Chudo Yudos were curious serpents with many heads on one body. They lived in the land of Ivan Popyaloff. Everyone knew that the dark was their doing. And all the hero warriors in all the broad land had tried to kill the great creatures, but none had succeeded. Now there dwelt there an old couple who had three sons. The two elder sons had their wits about them, but the third—*och*, the third was a simpleton, called Ivan Popyaloff. For twelve years Ivan had lain without stirring beside the stove in their kitchen. At last one day he rose. He shook himself, and two hundred pounds of ashes fell from his clothing.

" 'I, Ivan Popyaloff, will kill the Chudo Yudos," he said. 'Father, make me an axe that weighs one hundred pounds.'

"When Ivan had got the great axe he went out into the fields and flung it up into the air. Then he went home again. The next day he went again into the fields. He stood on the same spot from which he had flung the axe. He

*Little Nianya.

stood there with his head thrown well back. Suddenly the axe fell down from the sky. It hit Ivan on the forehead and it broke into two pieces.

"Ivan Popyaloff then went home and said to his father: 'Little Father, make me an axe that weighs two hundred pounds.' And when he had got such an axe, he went out into the fields and flung it aloft. The axe went flying up through the air. Three days and three nights passed. On the fourth day Ivan Popyaloff went to the spot. When the axe fell down again, it struck him on the knee, and the axe broke into pieces.

" 'Little Father, make me an axe that weighs three hundred pounds,' the youth said to his father. And again he went to the fields and flung the axe high, high up into the air. This axe was aloft for six days and six nights. On the seventh day, on the same spot, it fell down upon Ivan's forehead. This time the axe did not break; the youth's head bent beneath it.

" 'This axe will do for the Chudo Yudos,' said Ivan.

"So when he had got everything ready he set forth with his two brothers to fight the Chudo Yudos. The young men rode and rode, and at last there stood before them a hut set up on legs like those of a chicken. And somehow or other the brothers knew that this hut belonged to the dread Chudo Yudos.

"There was no one at home. So Ivan and his brothers went in to rest. Soon there rode up on horseback a great Chudo Yudo with three heads on his long body. As he drew near the hut, his steed stumbled, his hound howled, and his falcon cried out.

" 'How now,' roared the Chudo Yudo, 'why hast thou stumbled, O Steed? Why hast thou howled, O Hound? Why hast thou cried out, O Falcon?'

" 'How should I not stumble,' the steed replied, 'when inside the hut lie Ivan Popyaloff and his two brothers?'

" 'How should I not howl,' said the hound, 'when a foe is at hand?'

" 'How should I not cry out,' the falcon said, 'when your death awaits you?' Then the Chudo Yudo called out:

" 'Come forth, Ivan Popyaloff! Let us match our strength, one with the other.'

"Ivan stepped forth from out the hut, and they began to fight. With his terrible axe Ivan soon put an end to the Chudo Yudo with three heads. Then he went back again to rest inside the hut.

"Soon there rode up a Chudo Yudo with six heads on his long body. His steed stumbled, his hound howled, and his falcon cried out as he drew near the hut.

'How now, O Steed,' roared the great Chudo Yudo, 'why hast thou stumbled?'

Ivan soon put an end to the Chudo Yudo
with three heads.

And as before, the horse replied, 'How should I not stumble when inside that hut lie your enemy Ivan Popyaloff and his two brothers?'

"The Chudo Yudo called Ivan forth, and in their battle together Ivan soon put an end to the beast with six heads. The third Chudo Yudo was a great creature with twelve heads on his long body. He was mounted upon a horse with twelve wings, whose coat was of silver, and whose mane and tail were of gold.

"Ivan set forth to fight him. Soon he lopped off three of his heads. But straightway the creature touched the wounds with his finger and the heads flew back again to their places. With a blow at poor Ivan he drove him into the ground up to his knees. The youth then threw one of his gloves in at the window of the hut where his brothers were sleeping. But his brothers slept on.

"Next Ivan Popyaloff cut off six of the Chudo Yudo's twelve heads; but at one touch of the fiery fingers of the serpent, they grew back as before.

"Another great blow from the Chudo Yudo sent Ivan down into the ground up to the waist. He hurled his other glove into the house where his brothers were sleeping. But his brothers slept on.

"Again Ivan struck. This time he lopped off nine of the heads of the great Chudo Yudo. But again they grew back just as before. The Chudo Yudo was now weak. He could feel his strength going from him. And just then there flew overhead a black raven, croaking as he went past, 'Krof! Krof!'

" 'O Raven,' cried the Chudo Yudo, 'fly to the wives of myself and my brothers! Tell them the tale! Bid them come and eat up Ivan Popyaloff!'

"Ivan was now buried in the earth up to his armpits. He was at the very end of his force. But he threw his cap into the hut with all his might. The beams fell apart. The brothers awoke and rushed out to his aid. The dread Chudo Yudo with twelve heads was soon finished, and a great light broke forth over the land. The darkness was ended.

"But Ivan and his brothers were not yet quite safe. A little sparrow alighted upon Ivan's shoulder and whispered into his ear that the wives of the three dead Chudo Yudos were lying in wait for him on the way home.

" 'One has turned herself into a bed,' said the bird to Ivan. 'He who lies down upon it will be burned in red flames. Another has taken the form of a spring. He who drinks from it will drown in deep water. The third is now an apple tree whose fruit carries death. Beware, O Ivan Popyaloff!'

"As the three brothers traveled homeward, they soon

came to a green meadow in the midst of which there stood a broad golden bed.

" 'Let us turn our horses to graze,' said one of the brothers, 'and let us lie down to rest awhile on that soft bed.'

" 'Wait a bit, brothers,' Ivan cried out. He struck the bed with his axe, and blood dripped from its side. They went along farther until they came to an apple tree covered with fruit of silver and gold.

" 'Let us each have an apple,' the brothers said, halting. But Ivan held them back.

" 'Wait a bit, brothers,' he said. And he struck the tree with his axe. From the side of the trunk there gushed a stream of red blood.

"Farther along on their way, they rode up to a spring, and the brothers halted their steeds, saying:

" 'Let us have a drink of cold water.'

" 'Stop, my brothers,' Ivan cried. 'Wait a bit! Let us see! And he plunged his battle axe down into the water. Lo, the water also turned into blood!

" 'Now we can go on in peace, my brothers,' said Ivan Popyaloff. 'The three Chudo Yudos are dead. Their wives are no more. And through us has the darkness been lifted forever from our broad land.' "

The Frog Bride

OUTSIDE the double windows of the great country house the snow fell in swirling clouds of white. The wind howled and the birch tree at the side of the driveway flung its naked white branches first to this side, then to that, under the force of the gale.

Inside the house all was snug and warm. Everyone was busy about some task or other, and none thought of the blizzard that was raging over the fields and the forests, and that was smothering the peasants' huts with its vast white coverlid.

Kyril had gone down with old Uncle Feodor to watch the men in the carpenter shop, and Sonia was sitting beside her old nurse, their chairs drawn close to the tall porcelain stove in the corner of the linen room. Nianya was teaching her to make the fine crossed stitches with which the Russian peasant women adorn their clothes and their household linens.

"Oh dear, oh dear!" the little girl sighed. "It is all wrong again." She handed her bit of embroidery to the old woman, who began to untangle the bright red and blue threads.

"You do it for me, Nianyuska," the little girl begged. "You can do it so nicely. If you would, you could finish it in the wink of an eye."

"No, my little pigeon," the old nurse said, smiling down at the golden-haired child beside her. "I could not do it quite so quickly as that. I am not like the fairy nurses of Nadya the Frog Bride, in the old *skazka*."

"Tell me about them, Nianyuska," Sonia begged eagerly, "and I will try once again."

"Well," the old nurse began, "it all happened in I don't know what province of I don't know what land. But there once lived a Tsar and his Tsarina who had three fine sons. So splendid they were that no pen could write of them, and no tongue could tell.

"Well, one day the Tsar called his sons to him, saying, 'My dear children, you are now ready to marry. Let each one take up his bow and his arrow. Let him shoot an arrow far, far into the air. And on the spot where it falls, let him there find his bride.'

"So they shot, each one an arrow in a different direction. The first arrow fell below the tower of a nobleman's daughter. The second dropped on the stairway of a rich merchant's house, just at the feet of a beautiful maiden. But the arrow of the third son—*och*, my little pigeon, it dropped into a marsh, and a croaking frog caught it in her wide mouth as it fell.

" 'What shall I do?' cried Boris, the third son, whose arrow this was. 'How can I take a frog for my wife? A croaking thing like her is not worthy to be the bride of a prince.'

" 'Take her all the same, my son,' the Tsar said. 'We must believe that Heaven means her for your bride.'

"So the Tsar's sons took their brides. The eldest one wed the nobleman's daughter. The second one took the daughter of the rich merchant, while Boris, the third son, welcomed into his palace the croaking frog from the marsh. Then one day the Tsar called his three sons before him.

" 'Let your wives each bake for me by tomorrow morning a sweet white cake,' he said to them.

"Boris Son-of-the-Tsar went back to his palace sorry and sad, his head hanging low.

"'*Kva! Kva!*' croaked his Frog Bride. 'Why are you so sad, Boris Son-of-the-Tsar? Has your father treated you badly?'

"'How should I not be sad?' the young prince replied. 'My father has ordered that you shall make a sweet white cake for him before morning comes.'

"'Do not worry, Son-of-the-Tsar!' the Frog Bride croaked harshly. 'Lie down and rest! Morning is always wiser than evening.'

"As soon as the Tsar's son was asleep, the Frog Bride threw off her ugly frog's skin. And behold, she was a maiden, lovely and fair. You see, little pigeon, this Frog Bride was really Nadya the Fairy, the daughter of Kost-chey the One-Who-Never-Dies.

"Nadya stepped out on the wooden balcony of her chamber and cried in a loud voice, 'Oh, my fairy nurses! Gather about me! Put yourselves to work quickly, and bake for me a cake sweet and white, such as I used to eat in the palace of my old father!'

"Well, when Boris Son-of-the-Tsar awoke the next morning, lo, there stood before him a cake sweeter and whiter than one can imagine. Never has there been such a cake save in the *skazki*.

"The Tsar thanked Boris for the cake which he brought him. Then he gave a second order to his three sons.

" 'Let each of your wives weave for me a fine silken carpet, and let each one be finished by tomorrow morning!' he commanded.

Boris returned to his Frog Bride sorry and sad, his head hanging low.

" '*Kva! Kva!*' the Frog Bride croaked harshly. 'Why are you so sad, Boris Son-of-the-Tsar?'

" 'How should I not be sad, O Croaking One?' the Prince replied. 'My father, the Tsar, has commanded you to weave him a fine silken carpet, and it must be finished by morning.'

" 'Do not worry, Son-of-the-Tsar,' the Frog Bride replied. 'Lie down and rest. Morning is always wiser than evening.'

"And as before, the Frog Bride threw off her frog skin. She called her nurses to her and ordered that they weave a silk carpet such as that upon which she had sat in the home of Kostchey, her father. No sooner were the words spoken than it was done. In the morning the Tsar's son awoke to find spread out before him such a carpet as never was, save in the *skazki*. It was woven of silk and embroidered in fine silver and gold.

"The Tsar thanked Boris for the wonderful carpet and spoke again to his sons, ordering them to present themselves with their wives at the court the next day.

So they shot, each one an arrow in a different direction.

"Boris went back to his palace, sorry and sad, his head hanging low.

"'*Kva! Kva!*' croaked his Frog Bride. 'Why so sad, Boris Son-of-the-Tsar? Did your father speak harshly?'

"'How should I not be sad, O Croaking One?' cried the Prince. 'My lord and father has ordered me to appear with you before him and the whole court on the morrow. How shall I dare to show you there, my Frog Bride?'

"'Do not be sad, Son-of-the-Tsar,' the Frog Bride replied. 'You shall go ahead by yourself. I shall come after you. When you hear the rumbling of wheels, you must say to the court, 'It is my Frog Bride who arrives. She rides in her carriage, a little box upon wheels.'

"So it was done. The older brothers presented themselves at the Tsar's court with their beautiful wives, so richly adorned and so brilliantly dressed. And what fun they made of their poor younger brother!

"'Well, brother,' they said, sneering, 'you have come without your wife! You should have brought her, even if you had to carry her in your handkerchief. Where in the world did you ever get such a beautiful creature? You must have had to search all of the marshes to find such a great prize.'

"Just then a rumbling and rattling was heard in the courtyard. The whole palace shook. The guests were alarmed. They jumped up from their seats, wondering what it could be. But Boris Son-of-the-Tsar said to them calmly:

" 'Do not fear, gentlemen! It is only my Frog Bride who arrives. She rides in her carriage, a little box upon wheels.'

"All rushed to the windows. And behold, there was seen approaching a golden chariot drawn by six flying horses. It drew up at the entrance, and from it there stepped forth Nadya the Fairy, so brilliant and dazzling that one cannot imagine her beauty. Never has there been heard of a maiden so lovely except in the old fairy tales. She took the bewildered Boris by the hand and led him into the court. Before the vast sideboards of oak they stood eating and drinking. The other guests began to enjoy themselves also; but all eyes were fastened upon the lovely bride of Boris Son-of-the-Tsar.

" The wives of the two older princes watched her every movement. They saw that she drank only part of her glassful and she poured the rest into the palm of her left hand. And when she ate of the cooked swan, she hid the tiny bones in the palm of her right hand. The other two brides wondered, but they made haste to do likewise.

"Well, Nadya the Fairy entered the ballroom by the side of her husband, Boris Son-of-the-Tsar. She stretched out her left hand and lo, there before them all was a beautiful lake. She next stretched forth her right hand, and behold, on the lake there were seen swimming snowy white swans. The guests wondered and marveled, and everyone admired Nadya the Fairy.

"You can imagine, my child, that the two other brides were jealous. They hastened to stretch out their left hands also. But no lake appeared. The only thing that happened was that the angry guests were sprinkled all over with water. Then the other two brides stretched out their right hands, just as Nadya the Fairy had done. But no snowy white swans were to be seen. The only thing that happened was that a bone fell into the eye of the Tsar.

"*Och*, wasn't he angry! He chased them away without drum or trumpet to mark their departure."

Kostchey the One-Who-Never-Dies

"IS THAT all the story, Nianya?" Sonia asked, her blue eyes round with wonder at the marvelous tale.

"No, little pigeon," the old nurse said smiling, "that is not all. But how can I finish the tale if you do not do your work? Not one stitch have you put into your canvas since I gave it back to you."

"I will, Nianyuska! I will sew," the little girl pleaded. "Only tell me the rest." And she bent over her bit of canvas with its red and blue threads.

"Well, then, my darling," Nianya took up the tale again. "You can imagine that Boris Son-of-the-Tsar was overjoyed to find out that his wife was so charming. And a great idea came to him. He left the court room. He ran back to his palace, and there he found the frog's skin which his bride had taken off. He burned it in the great stove, thinking that now his wife would always have the beautiful form of Nadya the Fairy.

"But when Nadya returned home, she looked about for her frog skin. She searched and she searched. Nowhere could she find it. She grew worried and sad, and tears came to her eyes.

" 'What have you done, Boris, O Boris Son-of-the-Tsar?' she cried in distress. 'If you had waited but a little while longer, I should have been yours forever and ever. But now I must go. Farewell, my husband! Seek me in three times nine lands, in the thirtieth empire, in the palace of my father, Kostchey the One-Who-Never-Dies! There you may find me." And before Boris could take a single step towards her, Nadya the Fairy had changed herself into a snowy white swan and had flown out of the open window up into the sky.

Then indeed did Boris weep. He knelt down and prayed to God in Heaven. Then he turned himself around and around three times and he set forth over the land, going always straight ahead. Was it near? Was it far? Was the time long? Was it short? I do not know. But this I do know: At last Boris Son-of-the-Tsar met an old man. Oh, my little pigeon, he was a very old man.

" 'Hail, good young Prince,' said the Old Man. 'What do you seek? Where are you going, so sorry and sad?' And Boris Son-of-the-Tsar told the old man his story.

" '*Och*, Son-of-the-Tsar, why ever did you burn the frog's skin? Did you not know that Nadya the Fairy is the daughter of Kostchey the One-Who-Never-Dies? Her father was angry with Nadya because he feared she was becoming more skilled in magic than he. He changed her into a frog, and he commanded that she should wear a frog's skin for three whole years. The three years were nearly up when you spoiled it all. But I will help you, Boris Son-of-the-Tsar. Take this ball of golden thread. Throw it down on the ground! And where it rolls, follow!'

"Well, Boris thanked the Old Man and followed the golden ball as it rolled along over the land. He was just crossing the broad plain when he met a bear.

" 'Hm,' he said aloud, 'I think I will kill this bear.'

" 'Oh, do not kill me, Son-of-the-Tsar!' the bear cried out. 'Some day or other I may do you a service.'

" 'Well,' Boris said, 'I will not kill you,' and he went on his way, following the golden ball as it rolled on over the land. Suddenly he looked up at the sky, and there above him he saw an eagle flying along. Boris put his gun to his shoulder. He was about ready to shoot, when all at once the eagle spoke to him thus:

" 'Do not kill me, Son-of-the-Tsar! Some day or other, I may do you a service.'

"Boris did not want to let the eagle go, but still he did not shoot him. 'Well, I will not shoot you,' said Boris, and he went on his way, following the golden ball that rolled on and on before him. Farther along a wolf ran out of the forest. Again he raised his gun to his shoulder. Again he was all ready to shoot. But the wolf spoke to him thus:

" 'I pray you, Son-of-the-Tsar, do not kill me! I may be of help to you some day or other.' So Boris let the wolf go, and he went on and on until he came to the blue sea. There on the shore he found a great sturgeon that had been washed up on the sand. The fish lay gasping for breath, and all at once it called out to the young prince:

" 'Oh, Boris Son-of-the-Tsar, take pity upon me! Throw me back into the water! Then some day or other I will be of service to you.' The Tsar's son picked up the sturgeon and threw him into the sea. And he went on over the land.

"Well, the golden ball led Boris at last to a tiny hut that stood up on four chicken's legs and that turned round and round. Boris spoke to the hut, saying:

" 'Little hut! Little hut! Stand still before me, with

your face to my face and your back to the sea!' And the
little hut that rested on chicken's legs stood still before
the Tsar's son.

"The young man went in. There on the stove lay an old
woman. A Baba Yaga* she was, with skinny legs and a
nose that almost touched the roof of her hut.

" 'Hail, fine young man,' the Baba Yaga spoke from her
place on the stove. 'Why have you come to pay me a
visit?'

" 'Well, Baba Yaga,' the Tsar's son replied, 'if I am such
a fine young man, you may begin by cooking me food, by
giving me drink, and by heating a good hot steam bath for
me.' The old woman with the skinny legs and long nose

*Witch.

"Oh, Boris Son-of-the-Tsar, take pity upon me!
Throw me back in the water!"

hopped down from the stove. She gave the prince food, and poured him his drink and set about making ready the good hot steam bath. In the meanwhile Boris Son-of-the-Tsar told her his sad story and of his weary hunt for his Frog Bride.

" 'I know Nadya the Fairy,' the Baba Yaga said, nodding her head. 'She is with her father, Kostchey the One-Who-Never-Dies. It is a long journey there and it is a difficult journey, Boris Son-of-the-Tsar. Nor will it be easy, once you have reached the palace of Kostchey. For he keeps his daughter shut up, a prisoner, and he will not let her go.'

" 'I shall kill him,' cried the brave Boris, 'and then I shall set her free!'

" 'That is not so easy, my fine falcon,' said the Baba Yaga. For Kostchey is indeed the One-Who-Never-Dies. His death lies in a little needle. The needle is enclosed in an egg. The egg is inside a duck. The duck is inside a hare. The hare is shut up in a chest. And the chest is lodged high in the branches of a tall oak tree.'

"The Baba Yaga told Boris just where this tall oak tree stood. And the young man set forth again over the land. I do not know whether he walked for a long time or a short time. But at last he came to the tall oak with the casket lodged high in its branches.

" 'How shall I ever reach the casket, so high there in the branches of this tall oak tree?' Boris said to himself.

"And just then there came out of the forest the very same bear whose life the young prince had spared. The bear uprooted the oak tree so that it fell down to the ground. The chest fell with the oak, and it burst into pieces. Boris Son-of-the-Tsar rushed to the oak, but before he could reach it the hare ran out of the chest and fled away over the land.

" 'How ever shall I catch that hare?' Boris said to himself sadly. But just then the wolf whose life the Tsar's son had spared ran out of the bushes. It dashed after the hare and soon brought it back and laid it down at the feet of the prince. Boris cut the hare open with his sharp hunting knife. But before he could stop it, out of the hare flew the duck.

" 'How ever shall I get hold of the duck?' Boris exclaimed. He shot at it with his gun, but alas, his shot missed. Just then there came flying across the blue sky the eagle whose life Boris had spared.

"Well, the eagle flew fast, fast after the duck. On and on they flew until they were just over the sea. There the duck let drop the egg into the blue waters. Boris Son-of-the-Tsar burst into tears when he saw the precious egg go down under the waves.

" 'How ever shall I get the egg!' he cried aloud, as he ran back and forth along the sea shore. Suddenly out of the waters there swam the very sturgeon whose life he had spared. And in his great mouth he carried the egg!

"Boris took the egg and broke it wide open. Inside he found the tiny needle he sought, and he snapped it quickly in two. Then he made his way back to the palace where his bride, Nadya the Fairy, was waiting for him. Her father could no longer be called the One-Who-Never-Dies. For, as the old Baba Yaga had told, in the needle in the egg in the duck in the hare in the casket in the oak tree, Kostchey's death lay. And when the needle was broken, Kostchey's long life was ended, and Nadya the Fairy was free to return home with her husband, Boris Son-of-the-Tsar.

"My father knew this tale to be true, my little dove. He was present at the feast which the Tsar gave when his son returned with his bride. My father said that he drank much beer and *kvass*.* But it all ran down his beard and none of it went into his mouth."

*A sweet drink.

Clever
Semiletka

"OH, NIANYA, Nianyuska, I'm tired of lessons and lessons all day long," Kyril cried one winter afternoon as he came running with his sister into the room of his old nurse.

"First we had our French and our history with Mademoiselle," said Sonia with a sigh. Then geography and English with Miss. And this afternoon my piano lesson and practice."

"I had to do twice as much German as usual with Herr Schmidt today, too," Kyril said in disgust. "Now they have all gone to drink tea in the drawing room with the aunts and the cousins. At last we are free."

"*Na, na,* my doves, you must not speak so," the old

woman chided, shaking her head so hard that the ends of her bright headkerchief fairly danced on her shoulders. "What should you do in St. Petersburg when you are older, if you had not had all these lessons! What boobies you would appear if you could not speak German and English and French! They tell me Russian words are scarce ever heard in the drawing rooms of the fine Petersburg folk. Besides, it serves one well to be clever. It was only because she was so clever that poor Semiletka became a Tsarina."

"Wait, Nianya dear, until I pull my chair closer, and then you shall tell us about Semiletka," Sonia cried, delighted at the prospect of a new *skazka*.

"Well, long ago," the old woman began, "before your grandfathers had learnt their lessons, and before their grandfathers had been born, there once were two brothers. One was a rich peasant. The other was poor. The poor peasant's wife died, leaving him with a daughter, a good clever maid, whom they called Semiletka.

"One day Semiletka's rich uncle made her a present. He gave her a little heifer calf, puny and sick; so thin indeed was it that no one thought it would live. Semiletka brought the calf water and food. She took it into her hut, and she made it a bed close to the stove. She tended it herself by night and by day. And the calf began to grow and to grow. It became fat and round, and it grew into a healthy cow that at last gave birth to a calf.

"Well, one day the daughters of her rich uncle came to visit Semiletka. When they saw the healthy cow with her fine calf, they could not believe that it was the same puny heifer which their father had given to Semiletka.

"At home once again her cousins told the news to their father, who decided to try to get the heifer back again for himself. He went to his brother and demanded the cow. His brother refused, saying that it now belonged to his daughter, Semiletka.

" 'Well, then give me the calf,' said the greedy rich brother.

" 'No,' Semiletka replied; 'the cow is mine, so her calf is mine, too.'

" 'I gave you the heifer,' her uncle declared, 'but I did not mean that you should keep the calves.'

"But her father would not let Semiletka give up either the cow or its calf. He quarreled and quarreled with his rich brother. No peace did they have. At last they decided to go to the Tsar and let him settle the matter. The Tsar listened to their tale and then he said:

" 'We shall decide it this way. I shall give you each three riddles, and he whose answer is best shall have both the heifer and her calf. To begin with, guess me this: What is

The Tsar listened to their tale.

it that, in all the wide world, there is nothing so swift? Go home and bring me the answer tomorrow.'

"The peasants returned to their homes. The poor man hung his head. He thought and he thought what reply he should make. And as he entered his hut, he called Semiletka to him, saying:

" 'Ah, daughter, my daughter, the Tsar has demanded that I should tell him what it is that, in all the wide world, there is nothing so swift. What shall I tell him? If I do not guess right, he will give my brother our heifer.'

" 'Go to bed, Little Father,' Semiletka replied. 'Do not torment yourself! Morning is always wiser than evening.' So the poor peasant climbed up on the warm stove and went off to sleep. At dawn his daughter woke him, saying:

" 'Get up, dear Little Father, it is time to go to the Tsar. Go and tell him that in all the wide world there is nothing so swift as the thoughts that fly through our heads.'

"The peasant arose. He went forth to the Tsar's palace, and as he entered the courtyard, his brother came also.

" 'What is it that, in all the wide world, there is nothing so swift?' the Tsar demanded of the rich peasant. The rich peasant hurried to speak:

" 'Why, in my stable at home I have a horse so swift that no other can pass it. Surely in the whole world there could be nothing swifter than he.'

" 'The Tsar laughed at this answer. 'What will you say to this riddle, O peasant?' he said to the poor brother.

" 'In all the wide world, O Tsar, there is nothing so swift as the thoughts that fly through our heads,' the poor peasant said, as Semiletka had taught him. The Tsar was surprised at the poor peasant's answer.

" 'Who told you to say that?' he asked.

" 'My daughter, clever Semiletka,' the peasant replied.

" 'Good!' said the Tsar. 'Now for the second riddle: What is it that, in all the wide world, there is nothing so fat?'

"The two brothers returned again to their homes. The poor peasant hung his head. He thought and he thought what reply he should make. And he called to his daughter to come to his aid.

" 'The Tsar has demanded what it is that, in all the wide world, there is nothing so fat. What should that be? Oh, what shall I say?'

" 'Do not fret, Little Father,' said Semiletka. 'Go to bed and to sleep! Morning is always wiser than evening.'

"Snug and warm on the stove the poor peasant slept until the day broke. Then his daughter woke him, saying:

" 'Get up, Little Father! Go to the Tsar! Tell him that, in all the wide world, there is nothing so fat as the fat of the land.'

"Again the poor peasant stood with his rich brother before the Tsar. And again the Tsar spoke.

" 'What is it, O peasants, that in all the wide world, there is nothing so fat?' he asked. And the rich peasant answered.

" 'At my house, O Tsar, I have a fat pig than which there is nothing fatter in all the wide world.' The Tsar laughed at this and waited to hear the answer of the poor brother.

" 'O Tsar,' said the man, 'in all the wide world there is nothing so fat as the fat of the land.' The Tsar was astonished.

" 'Who taught you to speak thus, O peasant?' he cried.

" 'It was my daughter, clever Semiletka,' said the man.

" 'That is well,' the Tsar answered. 'Now for the third riddle! What is it that, in all the wide world, there is nothing so pleasant?'

"A third time the two brothers returned to their homes. A third time the poor peasant entered his hut in deepest despair, and he called to his daughter to help him in his trouble.

" 'O Semiletka,' he said, 'the Tsar has demanded that I tell him tomorrow what it is that, in all the wide world, there is nothing so pleasant. What shall I say? If I do not guess right, my brother will take our cow and our calf.'

" 'Go to bed, Little Father!' said Semiletka. 'Do not torment yourself. Morning is always wiser than evening.'

"And so the man slept soundly in his warm place upon the stove until morning came. Then Semiletka awoke him.

" 'Get up, Little Father!' she cried. 'Go to the Tsar and tell him that in all the wide world there is nothing so pleasant as sweet sleep, for in sleep all our troubles and worries are forgotten.'

"The man hopped down from the stove and went off to find the Tsar. His brother was there also, and together they stood ready to answer the third riddle.

" 'What is it that, in all the wide world, there is nothing so pleasant?' the Tsar demanded of them.

" 'A soft-spoken woman,' the rich brother replied. The Tsar smiled and turned to hear the answer of the poor peasant. That one replied as his daughter, Semiletka, had taught him:

" 'In all the wide world, O Tsar, there is nothing more pleasant than sweet sleep, for in sleep all our troubles and worries are forgotten.'

" 'Who taught you to answer thus, O wise peasant?' the Tsar asked.

" 'My daughter, the clever Semiletka,' the man replied proudly. 'In all of your kingdom there is not a maid like her.'

" 'It is well,' said the Tsar. 'The calf and the heifer are yours. But I desire to see your daughter, this clever Semiletka. I think I can give her a riddle that even she cannot guess. Tell her to come to me on the morrow neither afoot nor on horseback, neither in chariot nor sleigh, neither dressed nor undressed. And let her bring me a present that I cannot give back to her.'

"The poor peasant returned home, half glad and half sad. With joy he told Semiletka that the calf and the heifer were theirs. But then he began to weep bitter tears.

" 'Ah, my daughter,' he said, 'our end is near. The Tsar commands that you come to him tomorrow, neither afoot nor on horseback, neither in chariot nor sleigh, neither dressed nor undressed, and that you bring him a gift that he cannot give back to you. *Och*, what shall we do, what shall we do?'

" 'Do not fret, Little Father. Climb up on your bed. Morning is always wiser than evening,' said the clever maid, Semiletka.

"The next morning Semiletka awoke her father at dawn. She took off her clothes and rolled herself in a fish net. In this her father carried her on his back to the palace, and so she presented herself to the Tsar.

" 'I have come as you ordered, O Tsar,' Semiletka cried, 'neither afoot nor on horseback, neither in chariot nor sleigh, neither dressed nor undressed, and I have brought you a gift that you cannot return to me. Stretch forth your hand that I may give it to you.'

"The Tsar held out his hand. And the maiden put in it a young pigeon which straightway flew up into the air and out of the window. Indeed, the Tsar could not give back her gift to the maiden. The Tsar was delighted. He found Semiletka even more clever than her father had said, and she pleased him so much that he made her his bride. Together they lived a long happy life because they chose good and put evil behind them."

A Winter's Tale

"NO COASTING today, Sonia; it's too cold to go out," said Kyril, as he stood with his sister at their playroom window looking out at the white world beyond the thick double panes. "Old Foka has just come in from the village. He says it is so cold that his eyelids froze tight together."

"Yes, my doves, Morosko the Frost King is abroad in the land," old Nianya declared as she straightened the table with its litter of paint boxes and books. "This is a day to stay within-doors. Be glad that you have a warm house to shut out the icy north wind. We should all like to seek summer and run away from the winter, like the Ox, and the Ram, and the Pig, and the Goose."

"Tell us that tale again, Nianyuska," begged Sonia.

"How many times have I told it to you already?" the old woman asked, smiling down at the girl's eager face.

"Oh, a thousand, Nianya dear," Sonia replied. "But I'd like to hear it again."

"Well, then, my dove, it all began in the autumn. An Ox was walking one day out in the forest when he met a Ram.

" 'Where are you going, Ram?' the Ox asked.

"I am seeking the summer and running away from the winter,' the Ram replied. 'Won't you come along with me?' So they started off together. A little farther along they met up with a Pig.

" 'Where are you going, Pig?' the Ox asked.

" 'I am seeking the summer and running away from the winter,' was the Pig's answer.

" 'Come along with us,' the Ox and the Ram said to the Pig. And so he went along, too. A bit farther on they met a Gray Goose.

" 'Where are you going, Goose?' they inquired.

" 'Well, I am seeking the summer and running away from the winter,' said the Gray Goose.

" 'Come along with us,' the animals cried. And so the Gray Goose went with them. They walked and they walked until they met a Cock.

" 'Hail, O Cock!' they cried out. 'Where are you going?'

" 'Seeking the summer and running away from the winter,' he too declared. He joined their party, and off they all went, seeking the summer and trying to run away from the winter.

"Along the roads through the forests and over the plains they walked on together. And as they walked, they talked of the cold winds and the ice and the snow that would soon come to cover the land.

" 'How now, my comrades!' the Ox said one day. 'The cold times draw near. Then where shall we warm ourselves? Let us all build a hut, or we shall freeze when winter comes.'

" 'No, friend,' said the Ram, 'I shall not trouble. I have a fur coat on my back. It will keep me warm without any hut.'

" 'As for me,' said the Pig, 'I have no fear of the frost and the cold. I shall dig myself a hole in the ground and shall be snug and warm there.'

" 'Why should I need a hut!' the Goose declared stoutly. 'I shall sit in the midst of a thick pine tree. I have two wings. One wing shall be my bed and the other my coverlid. So no cold can find me.'

"And I shall follow the lead of my good friend, the

Goose,' said the Cock, boasting. 'I shall not need a hut, however cold the winter may be.'

"The Ox was sad. He saw that he should have to build his hut all by himself. 'Well, my friends,' he said to the other animals, 'do as you think best. But I shall build a log hut for myself.' And build a log hut he did, and he went to live in it.

"That winter was cold. As cold as today and colder, my little pigeons. The frost pinched and nipped. It found its way through the fur coat on the Ram's back, so that he ran to knock at the door of the Ox's hut.

" 'Let me come in, O Ox, and warm myself at your fire. I am so cold.'

" 'No, Ram,' said the Ox; 'you have a warm fur coat on your back. You do not need a house. You can spend the winter outdoors. I will not let you in.'

" 'Well, Ox,' said the Ram, 'if you will not let me in, I shall rush at the door and butt it down with my hard head. Then it will only be the colder for you.'

"The Ox thought and thought. He saw plainly that he must give in, for he too might freeze to death in the cold if his door were burst open. So he let the Ram in.

"Soon the Pig also came to knock on the door of the hut and asked to be let in.

" 'Ox, O Ox, I am chilled to my very bones. Let me

come in and warm myself in your hut,' the Pig cried between his chattering teeth.

" 'No, Pig,' said the Ox, 'you cannot come in. You can
dig yourself a hole down in the ground where you can
keep snug and warm. I will not let you in.'

" 'Well, Ox,' the Pig threatened, 'if you do not let me
in, I shall root under your house and it will all tumble
down.'

"There was nothing to be done about it. The Ox had to
let the Pig in. Then the Goose and the Cock knocked at
the door of the hut.

" 'Brother, let us come in and warm ourselves in your
hut,' the two creatures cried.

" 'No, I will not let you in," the Ox declared angrily.
'Each of you has two wings. One shall serve as your bed
and the other your coverlid. No cold can find you.'

" 'Well, then,' said the Goose, 'I shall peck all the moss
from between the logs of your hut and let in the cold air.'

" 'And I,' said the Cock, 'will fly up on your roof and
tear down all the thatch. You yourself will only be the
colder for it if you do not let me in.'

"What could the Ox do? He had to let in both the
Goose and the Cock. And they all lived there together in
the little log hut, warm and content.

"One day the Cock was so happy that he began to sing his loud song. And just then a Fox ran past the hut. She heard the loud song and thought to herself what a fine dish the singer would make for her dinner. She looked in at the window and saw the Ram and the Ox.

" 'How shall I get the Cock?' the Fox thought to herself. 'I must have aid. I could not manage alone.' So she went on to find the Bear and the Wolf who lived in the forest near by.

" 'My dear comrades,' the Fox cried to them, 'I have found food for all three of us. In a little hut near by are living an Ox, a Ram, and a Cock. You, Bear, you shall have the Ox; for you, Wolf, the Ram; and for me myself, the Cock.'

" 'Good, good!' said the Bear and the Wolf. 'Well done, Friend Fox. We shall not forget what we owe you. Let us go now and eat them.' So they went on across the snow until they came to the log hut. Then the Fox said to the Bear:

" 'You, Bear, open the door, and I shall go in first and eat up the Cock.'

"The Bear opened the door. The Fox jumped into the hut. The Ox saw her and crushed her against the log wall with his great horns. The Ram ran to butt her with his

The fox thought what a fine dish the singer would
make for her dinner.

hard head. The Pig began worrying her. The Goose pecked at her eyes, and the Cock flew up on a perch near the stove, crying, 'Bring her to me! Bring her to me!' It did not take them long to make an end of that Fox, I can tell you, my doves.

"Out-of-doors the Bear and the Wolf grew uneasy. 'Why is it that she takes so long a time to eat up a Cock?' the Wolf said to the Bear. 'Open the door, Bear, and let me go in.'

"The Bear opened the door. The Wolf jumped into the hut. The Ox crushed him with his horns. The Ram butted him with his hard head. The Pig worried him, and the Goose pecked at his eyes, while the Cock cheered them on from his perch near the stove. Thus came the end of the hungry Wolf.

"The Bear waited and waited outside the door. 'Why is he so long about killing a Ram? I had best go and see,' he said to himself. So he opened the door and stepped inside the hut. The Ox crushed him against the log wall. The Ram butted him with his hard head. The Pig and the Goose worried and pecked at him, while the Cock on his perch cried, "Bring him to me! Bring him to me!'

"With a mighty struggle the Bear got away from them all. He rushed out of the hut, and he ran and he ran without looking back. And the Ox was glad, after all, that he had with him such good friends as the Ram and the Pig, the Gray Goose and the Cock. So they all went on living and thriving in the little log hut, waiting just as you and I are waiting, my little pigeons, for spring to come to the land."

The
Little Feather
of the
Splendid Falcon

OLD Nianya was busy in her own little room one winter afternoon when the two children knocked on her door in the hope of persuading her to tell them a *skazka*. They found her kneeling in front of her trunk, the huge old-fashioned box which always stood in the corner nearest the window and in which she kept all her belongings.

The old woman had been searching for some treasure or other and had taken out almost half the contents of the trunk. The floor about her was piled high with bits of lace and embroidery, with tiny boxes and bundles, with photographs and odds and ends that always fascinated Kyril and Sonia.

"What is this, Nianyuska?" Kyril asked, picking up a box filled with bright-colored feathers.

"*Tscha*," said the old nurse, taking it from him and running her worn fingers over the shining feathers of blue, orange, and green. "Those are the feathers from a pheasant that your father shot in the forest these many years gone. I keep them always because they are so pretty and bright. I am sure the feathers of Pheniste the Splendid Falcon were not finer than these, though the *skazka* does say that his shone like the fire."

"That is the story you shall tell us today," Sonia declared, waving one of the gay feathers.

"Very well, Little Princess," Nianya said, smiling and entering into the game. "Like the maid in the story of Pheniste the Splendid Falcon, you wave the magic feather and behold, your wish comes true. I will tell you the tale.

"Once there lived a man who had three daughters. The two elder daughters were selfish and vain, and they loved to deck themselves out in fine clothes. Olga, the youngest, however, preferred to busy herself about the house, although of the three she was the fairest. Her face was more beautiful than pen can describe or story can tell of.

"One day the father was going to town to visit the fair. 'What shall I bring you, my daughters?' he said to the three maidens.

" 'For me, Little Father, a robe of red silk,' the eldest one said.

" 'And for me, a silk kerchief to wear on my head,' said the second daughter.

" 'As for me, I should like a little silver-gilt flower,' the youngest daughter declared.

"The father easily found the silken robe and the silk kerchief, but in all the booths at the fair he saw no silver-gilt flower such as his youngest daughter desired. However, on the road homeward he met up with an old man who carried in his arms just the flower he sought.

" 'How much for your flower?' the father inquired.

" 'It is not for sale,' said the old man. 'But I will make you a present of it, if you will give me your youngest daughter as a bride for my son.'

" 'Who may your son be, then, Old Man?' asked the father.

" 'He is Pheniste the Splendid Falcon,' was the reply. 'By day he flies through the clouds; by night he comes down to earth as a handsome young prince.'

"What to do? The father scratched his head thoughtfully. If he refused, he would disappoint his dear daughter, Olga. But if he consented, God alone knew what sort of a bridegroom he was getting for her. At last he decided to run the risk and to accept the silver-gilt flower. He took

it, and straightway the old man disappeared. The father
was troubled. There was something about all this that he
did not understand.

" 'Here is your gift, dear little daughter,' he said to Olga
as he handed her the pot with its silver-gilt blossom. 'But
your gilt flower does not please me. It does not please me
at all.'

" 'Why not, dear Little Father?' Olga asked, wondering.
Her father took her aside and told her in secret how he had
met the old man and how he had promised her hand to his
son, Pheniste the Splendid Falcon.

" 'Do not worry, Little Father,' Olga replied. 'Who can
tell? Perhaps Pheniste the Splendid Falcon will please us
when he flies down to earth.' And she shut herself up in
her own little chamber. She opened her window wide to
the blue sky. On the sill she placed the pot with its silver-
gilt flower. And she sat down beside it, waiting and waiting.

"Just as the sun was dropping down behind the dark
forest, there came flying from somewhere or other a
Splendid Falcon with bright-colored feathers that shone
like the fire. To Olga's dormer window he came. He lit
upon the sill. Then he flew into the room. Hardly had his
feet touched the floor when he became a prince, so splendid
and handsome as never has been except in the fairy tales.

The maiden was about to scream in her fright, but the young man spoke to her gently.

" 'Do not fear, my dear bride,' he said. 'Each evening until our wedding I will come so to visit you at the sunset. As soon as you place your little silver-gilt flower here on the sill, I will appear. See, I have a gift for you. It is this feather from the wing of Pheniste the Falcon. Take it and treasure it. Step out on your balcony and wave it about. Whatever you wish, that shall be done.'

"The Splendid Falcon embraced the beautiful maiden. He was so handsome and his manner so fine that Olga loved him at once. Then he flew away again, out of her open window.

"Each evening the maiden placed her little gilt flower upon her window sill. And each evening there flew from out the blue sky her Falcon Bridegroom. So seven days passed. Sunday came. The two elder daughters made themselves ready to go to the church. And they laughed at their sister, saying:

" 'We have our new silk gown and our new silk kerchief to wear, but you, you have nothing.' Olga shook her head, smiling.

" 'That makes no difference to me,' she said. 'I shall stay at home today.' But when her two sisters had departed, she went out on her balcony. She waved her little feather and made a wish just as her bridegroom had taught her. And, my little pigeons, all at once there appeared from I don't know where a splendid carriage of crystal, drawn by six prancing horses and accompanied by servants all dressed in gold lace. The maiden found herself clad in a gown of silver and gold and many fine jewels.

"At the church everyone turned to admire her great beauty and her fine clothing. 'See, a Tsar's daughter!' the people whispered to one another. After the Mass they stood at the church door to see her depart. At home once more, Olga took off her golden gown and waved her little feather again. Lo, all the splendor and the finery straightway disappeared. When her sisters came back they found her sitting beside her window just as they had left her.

" 'Ah, little sister,' they cried, 'you should have gone with us today. A Tsar's daughter came to Mass. She was so beautiful that one forgot everything else in looking at her.'

"So passed two weeks. So passed two Sundays. But on the second Sunday, by some chance or other Olga left a sparkling pin in her hair when she took off her fine clothes. And when her sisters returned from church they spied it at once. 'What have you there, sister?' they cried out in wonder. And from that moment on they tried to find out her secret.

"They watched Olga. They followed her. They listened at the door of her little chamber. And they soon discovered that a splendid falcon flew into her room every evening at sunset. One day the wicked sisters sprinkled her window sill with bits of sharp broken glass. They planted upon it needles and knife points, so that the Splendid Falcon should wound himself when he lit there.

"That evening Pheniste the Splendid Falcon flew down as usual from the blue sky. But he could not light upon the window sill as before. He cut his claws on the knives, and he hurt his tender legs on the sharp bits of glass. He grew very sad. He spread his bright wings and cried out to the maiden.

" 'Farewell, O Olga, my beautiful bride, never will you see me again in your chamber! Seek me across twenty-seven plains in the thirtieth kingdom! But long is the road and distant its end. You shall use sandals of steel; you shall break a staff of cast iron; you shall eat bread hard as stone —before you shall find me!'

"A heavy sleep fell suddenly upon the young maiden. And she slept and she slept until morning came. But still she remembered the words of Pheniste the Splendid Falcon. She made ready her packet, and she quitted her home to go out into God's world to seek her lost bridegroom. She walked and she walked, the poor beautiful maiden.

Through the deep forests she went, over the dry deserts and into the marshes whose water was rust-red.

"Did she go on and on for a long time or for a short time? That I do not know. But at last she found herself standing before a tiny hut. She knocked at the window and begged shelter for the night.

" 'Welcome, my dove,' said the old woman who opened the door of the hut. 'Where are you going?'

" 'Ah, Little Mother,' Olga cried, 'I seek my lost bridegroom, Pheniste the Splendid Falcon. Tell me where I shall find him.'

" 'That I cannot say,' said the old woman, 'but my sister can tell you. Take this ball of yarn. Let it roll on before you and it will show you the way.'

"Next morning, as Olga departed, the old woman gave her two gifts.

" 'This distaff of silver and this spindle of gold are my gifts for you,' she said to the girl. 'When you spin hemp upon them, gold thread will unroll. They will be of use to you when the time comes.'

"Olga thanked her and went along on her way, following the ball of yarn over the land to a second small hut. There she spent the night also. And when she departed, the second old woman gave her a silver tray and a small silver apple.

At last she found herself standing before a tiny hut.

" 'Long is the road that lies before you, my child,' the old woman said. 'Go on to the hut of my oldest sister. She can surely guide you better than I. Here, take my gifts! They will serve you when the time comes.'

"So Olga went on, farther and farther through I don't know what lands. The forest became blacker and blacker. The tips of the trees seemed to kiss the blue sky. At last her ball of yarn led her to a tiny hut, and there she spent the night with the third of the old sisters.

" 'It is a sad tale,' the third old woman said in reply to the girl's eager questions. 'Your bridegroom, Pheniste the Falcon, is about to marry the daughter of a great Tsar. The wedding day draws near. But perhaps I can help you. When you have passed through this forest, you must seat yourself upon the bank of the blue sea. Spin your golden thread with your silver distaff and your golden spindle. And if any should wish to buy them from you, do not take money for them. In exchange, demand only to see Pheniste the Falcon.'

"The girl went on, on, on. The forest became thinner. The trees became smaller. Then, behold, there was the blue sea, and in the distance was a city with towers of gold and houses of white. Olga sat down on the bank of the blue sea and began to spin golden thread with her silver distaff

and her golden spindle. Then along came the Tsar's daughter, followed by her attendants.

" 'Sell me your silver distaff and your spindle of gold, O Maiden,' said the Tsar's daughter. But Olga replied, 'O daughter of the Tsar, I cannot sell them. But I will give them to you for nothing, if only I may look upon Pheniste the Splendid Falcon.'

"The Tsar's daughter considered. Then she agreed that the maiden should go into his chamber while the Splendid Falcon was taking his rest after dinner.

"The Tsar's daughter put the silver distaff and the

golden spindle away in her tower. Then she gave the Falcon a drink of water mixed with strong sleeping herbs. Only when he had fallen into a deep sleep did she allow Olga to come into his chamber.

" 'Wake, wake, Splendid Falcon,' Olga cried out, as she bent, weeping over his pillow. 'I have come across twenty-seven plains to the thirtieth kingdom. I have used sandals of steel. I have broken a staff of cast iron. I have eaten bread hard as stone, always seeking and seeking for you, my beloved.'

"But the Prince did not wake up, and the Tsar's daughter led the maiden away. When at last Pheniste the Splendid Falcon arose from his rest, he rubbed his eyes, bewildered.

" 'I must have slept a long time,' he said to the Tsar's daughter. 'It seemed to me that someone was here, weeping and praying over my pillow.'

" 'It was only a dream,' the Tsar's daughter declared. 'I was here beside you all the time, brushing the flies away from your head.'

"The next day Olga sat again beside the blue water. She rolled her silver apple about upon her silver tray, as the Tsar's daughter came past. The Princess desired to buy this plaything also.

" 'Allow me to see Pheniste the Splendid Falcon once again,' said Olga, 'and I will give my silver tray and my silver apple to you.' The Tsar's daughter agreed, and again she gave to the Falcon a drink of strong sleeping herbs. But this time, as the weeping Olga bent over his pillow, a tear from her eyes fell down upon the cheeks of the young prince.

" 'What burned me?' cried the Falcon, jumping up from his couch.

" 'Beloved Falcon,' said Olga, 'I have come across twenty-seven plains, to the thirtieth kingdom. I have used sandals of steel. I have broken a staff of cast iron. I have eaten bread hard as stone, always seeking you, my well-beloved. Twice have I wept and prayed above your pillow. But you sleep on and on, and do not reply to my pleadings.'

"So great was the joy of Pheniste the Splendid Falcon at sight of the fair Olga that one can scarcely describe it. Olga told him her tale; how her sisters had plotted and how she had bargained with the Tsar's daughter. The Splendid Falcon loved her more than ever before. He kissed her sweet lips and then ordered that the bells in the palace tower should ring to assemble the princess and nobles.

" 'Tell me, my people,' he said when all were gathered below his balcony in the courtyard of the palace. 'Tell me which one of these maidens should become my bride: the one who has sold me or the one who has bought me?'

"With a mighty shout, with one voice, the people declared that Olga should become the bride of Pheniste the Falcon. The wedding was gay and the feast was fine. I can see it so well that it seems to me as though I had really been there and had drunk beer and honey with the wedding guests."

The Four Underground Kingdoms

T WAS Butter Week, the week before Lent began in Old Russia. Every day the two Russian children ate many *blini,* those delicious golden brown pancakes which they covered with hot melted butter. How good they tasted! To Kyril and Sonia *blini* always seemed better in Butter Week than at any other time. Perhaps this was because they knew they should not taste them at all during the Lenten fast which, in old Russia, lasted for seven weeks.

On this Sunday in Butter Week all in the great country house had gone to the church down in the village for the Forgiving Service. They had watched the priest in his robes kneel, facing the people, to beg their forgiveness for any wrong he might have done. Then, one by one, the children and their elders filed up and knelt down before the priest, asking for pardon and receiving his blessing. At the end of the service each one in the church turned to his neighbor and begged his forgiveness.

"Did you truly forgive every one, Nianya dear?" Sonia asked her old nurse that afternoon.

"How else should I be forgiven by God?" said the old woman. "Of course I forgave everyone, even that Varya down in the kitchen who has been calling me names when my back is turned."

"I try to forgive," Sonia said thoughtfully. "But I am not sure that I have truly forgiven Kyril for breaking my very best doll."

"Ah, but you must, my dove," Nianya said earnestly. "You have so little to pardon. Now if it had been a real wrong that your brother had done you like that which Prince Stepan forgave his wicked brothers in the tale of the Four Kingdoms, ah, that would be different."

"What was that, Nianyuska?" Sonia and Kyril cried together, speaking the very same words at the very same time in their eagerness to hear Nianya tell a new *skazka*.

"Well, *golub-chicki*, there once was a Tsar who had a beautiful wife called Anastasia of the Golden Hair. One day as the Tsarina walked in her garden, up came a great

Whirlwind and carried her off. The Tsar fell ill from grief. He sent for his sons and bade the two older ones go forth to seek their lost mother.

"The youngest son, Stepan, wished to go also. But at first the Tsar refused to give his consent. 'You, my dear son, must stay at home to comfort me in my loneliness,' he said to the youth. But Stepan was set upon going, and he begged and he pleaded. At last his father gave him his blessing, and he rode forth under the sun on his beautiful horse.

"Prince Stepan rode on and on. At last he came to the shore of a mighty ocean. As he looked over the blue waves, wondering which way to turn, there fluttered to earth thirty white doves who changed themselves into thirty beautiful maidens. All were lovely to look upon, but one there was even more beautiful than the others. The maidens took off their garments and plunged into the blue waters.

"While they were bathing, Prince Stepan hid the golden girdle that belonged to the most beautiful one of them all.

" 'Pray, give me my girdle, O Stepan Son-of-the-Tsar,' the maiden cried out when she discovered her loss.

" 'First you must tell me where I can find my mother, Anastasia of the Golden Hair,' said the young prince.

" 'Alas, that I do not know, O Son-of-the-Tsar, but the

little old woman who lives in yonder forest surely can help you,' the maiden replied. So Stepan gave her the girdle; and he rode and he rode until he came to a hut in the midst of the forest.

" 'Good-day, Little Mother,' he said to the Baba Yaga who opened the door.

" 'Good-day, good young man,' the Baba Yaga replied. 'Where do you go?'

" 'I seek my mother, Anastasia of the Golden Hair. Pray tell me where I can find her.'

" 'Take the highroad beside the blue sea,' said the Baba Yaga. 'There you will meet a bird with wings of silver and tail of gold. Follow its flight.'

"Along the highroad beside the blue sea Stepan came upon his two brothers, who decided that they would like to go along with him. And as the Baba Yaga had told, they soon saw a bird with wings of silver and tail of gold. And they followed its flight. The bird flew and flew. All at once it disappeared under a slab of iron that covered a great hole in the ground.

" 'Bless me, I pray you,' said Stepan to his brothers. 'I am going under the earth to follow the bird.' His brothers gave him their blessing, and they let him down into the hole by means of two long, long straps.

"Down, down, down he slid. It took no less than three hours to reach the bottom of the great hole. Then Stepan set out afoot across the underground kingdoms. He walked and he walked. He walked on and on.

"Suddenly there arose before him a splendid palace of copper. At its entrance were coiled two hissing serpents, bound fast by strong copper chains. Near-by was a well, and on the well was a pail, also of copper.

"Stepan dipped the copper pail into the well. He sprinkled the serpents with drops of its water. The hissing snakes lay themselves down, quiet and calm. The Prince passed safely between them and entered the palace. And there he met the beautiful Tsarina of the Copper Kingdom.

" 'Alas, good young man,' the Tsarina said in reply to Stepan's plea for assistance, 'I do not know where you shall find your mother, Anastasia of the Golden Hair. But my sister, the Tsarina of the Silver Kingdom, may be able to tell you. Take this copper ball and let it roll on before you to show you the way. And take this copper ring, so that you may not forget me. I, too, am a prisoner of the great Whirlwind. When you have found your dear mother, I pray you, take me back with you to the free country.'

"In the Kingdom of Silver, Prince Stepan found a palace even more beautiful. And the serpents guarding its doors

They soon saw a bird with wings of silver and
tail of gold.

were even more terrible. They were fastened with silver chains, and they lay near a well with a silver pail, hung upon a chain of silver. Stepan, the Tsar's son, sprinkled the serpents with water which he drew from the well near-by. And as before, they grew calm and allowed him to pass.

" 'Here it is, now, three years that the Whirlwind has held me his captive,' said the Tsarina of the Silver Kingdom to Stepan. 'Not in all that time have my eyes seen a Russian nor my ears heard a Russian, yet here is a Russian! What do you seek, good young man?'

" 'I seek my mother, Anastasia of the Golden Hair,' said Prince Stepan. 'Pray tell me where I can find her.'

" 'Ah, Stepan Son-of-the-Tsar,' the Tsarina replied, 'I do not know, but my elder sister, Elena the Beautiful, Tsarina of the Golden Kingdom, surely can help you. Take this silver ball and let it roll on before you to show you the way. And take this silver ring, so that you shall not forget to take me back with you to the free country.'

"The palace of the Golden Kingdom shone like a bright fire. At its entrance gates were two hissing serpents upon golden chains. And beside them was a well with a golden pail hung on a chain of pure gold. Stepan sprinkled the serpents and entered the palace. Elena the Beautiful came forth to meet him.

" 'Hail, good young man,' the Tsarina greeted Stepan.

'Is it your wish or is it Fate that brings you to us here?'

" 'It is my wish,' Stepan made reply. 'I seek my mother, Anastasia of the Golden Hair, whom the great Whirlwind carried away. Do you not know where I may find her?'

" 'How should I not know?' answered Elena the Beautiful. 'She lives near-by in the palace of the Great Whirlwind himself. Take this golden marble and let it roll on before you to show you the way. And take this golden ring, so that you shall not forget me. When you have rescued your mother, I pray you take me along with you back to the free country.'

" 'It shall be so,' Stepan promised Elena, and he went along, following the rolling marble of gold. He walked and he walked. And at last he came to the palace of the Great Whirlwind. It blazed like the sun, for it was studded with diamonds and many other fine jewels. And at its gates there were two serpents, each with six hissing heads. Stepan sprinkled the great snakes with the magic well water, and they lay themselves down, quiet and calm.

"In the Diamond Palace indeed, Stepan found his lost mother, seated on a high throne and wearing a crown.

" 'Ah, my dear son,' cried Anastasia of the Golden Hair, 'I fear you are not strong enough to vanquish the Great Whirlwind. Even the Spirits of the Mountains bow before his might. But we shall see. Come with me! Perhaps a trick will yet save us!'

"The Tsarina led the youth down into the cellar of the Diamond Palace, where there stood two great vats filled with sparkling water.

" 'Stepan, my son,' Anastasia said, 'these waters are magic. That on the right is the water of strength. That on the left is the water of weakness. He who drinks of the water of strength becomes a great warrior, while he who drinks the water of weakness loses all force. Let us change the vats quickly. That at the right, place it at the left. And that at the left, place it at the right. Perhaps by this trick we may yet best the Great Whirlwind.' And the Tsarina taught her son just what he must do when the Whirlwind arrived.

"Hardly had she finished when there came a rushing and roaring. The Tsarina hid Stepan behind her throne just as the Whirlwind flew into the palace. He touched the floor and changed himself into a mighty young man, carrying a battle-staff in his right hand.

" '*Pfui! Pfui! Pfui!*' he cried to the Tsarina. 'I smell a Russian. Someone has come from the free country to see you!'

" 'What do you say?' the Tsarina answered, trembling. "You must be in a dream.' But just then Stepan rushed forth from behind the throne and seized hold of the battle-staff of the Great Whirlwind.

" 'Let go, O Russian,' the Whirlwind roared. 'Let go! I will kill you!'

"And the Whirlwind threw himself out of the window and soared up into the sky, with Stepan holding tight to his battle-staff. They flew over the mountains and over the seas, but still the brave Stepan grasped the staff tightly. Around the whole of God's world they flew, but still the Prince held fast to the battle-staff.

"At last the Whirlwind grew tired. He dropped down into the cellar of the Diamond Palace for a drink of the magic water of strength. And as always, he drank from the vat that stood at the right, not knowing that the positions of the two waters had been changed. So while the Whirlwind drank of the water of weakness, Stepan hastened to drink of the water of strength. As he drank, the young Prince became the mightiest warrior in all the broad land.

"When Stepan saw that the Whirlwind was losing his force, he struck at him with his sword and he cut off his head. Then he sought out his mother to take her away. And he did not forget to set free the Tsarinas of the Three Kingdoms of Copper, Silver, and Gold.

"At the bottom of the great hole, Stepan tugged at the

straps. His brothers above pulled up, first, their mother, Anastasia of the Golden Hair, and next, Elena the Beautiful and her two lovely sisters. It was then Stepan's turn. But wicked thoughts came into the minds of his two brothers. 'If we leave him below,' they said to each other, 'then we can say that we ourselves rescued our mother and the Tsarinas.'

"So they cut the two straps into pieces and went away from the hole, leaving poor Stepan to wander about the underground kingdoms. He walked and he walked, and once again he came to the Diamond Palace of the Great Whirlwind. There on the window sill he discovered a flute. He put it to his lips and blew a few notes upon it. And all at once there stood before him a lame man and a man with only one eye.

" 'What is your need, Master?' they said to Stepan.

" 'I am hungry,' said Stepan, and to his amazement there stood ready before him a table covered with food fit for a tsar. After his dinner, Stepan felt sleepy. He blew on his flute, and when the strange pair appeared, he said, 'I am tired. I need a place to rest my head.' And lo, as he spoke, a soft bed stood beside him. After his nap Prince Stepan again blew upon his magic flute.

" 'Can you perform anything I may ask?' he said to the lame man and the man with only one eye.

" 'Anything!' was the reply. 'We are the slaves of the magic flute. As we served the dead Whirlwind, so will we serve you.'

"Prince Stepan commanded them to take him back again to his own kingdom. Hardly had he spoken the words than he found himself in his own city in the midst of the market place. And he hired himself to a cobbler, because he was not yet ready to make his presence known at the palace.

" 'You have come just in time,' the cobbler said. 'We are to have three great wedding feasts. The Tsar's sons are to wed Elena the Beautiful and one of her sisters. And the third strange Tsarina is to marry a noble.'

"That night Prince Stepan played once more upon his magic flute. He commanded his servants to make for him a pair of shoes more beautiful than ever had been before. The cobbler took these wonderful shoes next day to the market place, and there the Tsarina Elena spied them as she walked about with her sisters.

" 'What can that mean?' she cried. 'Such shoes as those are only found in the underground kingdoms. Surely it was the servants of the Whirlwind's magic flute that made these fine shoes. And she said to the cobbler. 'How is it, O Cobbler, that you have such shoes as these?'

" 'Oh, I can make anything,' the man replied, boasting.

He did not like to tell of his new helper who had made the shoes overnight.

" 'If that is true, I desire you to make me a marriage robe,' the Tsarina commanded. 'Let it be woven of gold and adorned with fine gems. And see to it that it be ready by tomorrow morning!'

"The poor cobbler was frightened. He knew he could not make such a fine marriage robe. He went home in fear, thinking his end was near. But Stepan comforted him, telling him that the marriage robe should be ready. And ready it was! For Stepan blew on his flute and bade his servants to make a marriage robe such as never was seen or heard of save in a *skazka*.

"When Elena the Beautiful saw the gold wedding gown, she forced the trembling cobbler to tell her the truth. 'Run! Fetch your helper!' she ordered. And when Stepen appeared, she knew him at once.

" 'Here is our true rescuer, O Tsar,' she said, leading Stepan before his wondering father. 'And here is my bridegroom. I will marry him only, for he it was that saved us.' She told how the wicked brothers had cut the straps and how they had forced her and her sisters to keep their evil secret.

"The Tsar wanted to punish the two wicked brothers. But the good Stepan begged their father to grant them his pardon. You see, my little pigeons, Stepan gladly forgave his wicked brothers, as all good people forgive those who sin against them.

"The feasting went on. Stepan married Elena the Beautiful, and everyone was happy and gay. Even the cobbler had plenty to eat and to drink.

The
Wonderful Beer
of
Poor Petrusha

S THIS evening wore on, Kyril and Sonia felt tired, but oh, so very happy. First, their dear mother and father had just come home from St. Petersburg with their trunks filled with presents. And second, tomorrow was Easter! Kyril and Sonia loved Easter even better than Christmas. It was such a gay, happy time. There was such feasting and merriment, and so many visitors came and went during the three-day celebration.

All day the Russian boy and girl had been busy. In the morning they had dyed great bowls of colored eggs for the Easter table. Throughout the afternoon they had run all over the great house, watching the preparations for the morrow's rejoicing.

In the kitchen they had seen the cook baking the Easter loaves which they called *"koulich"* and which looked so much like the round domes on the church down in the village. They had inspected each huge pyramid of white cheese, the sweet *"Pashka"* full of almonds and decorated with a raisin cross on its side. They had sniffed at the hams and the sausages and the other good things that were being cooked for the feast.

The great copper samovar, in which the hot water was always kept boiling for tea, shone even brighter than on other days, and down in the cellar the menservants had been bottling a barrel of *kvass*, that drink so beloved of all Russian people.

Now evening had come. Kyril and Sonia were resting after their dinner. They were trying their best to keep wide awake, for they were to go with their parents to the Easter-eve midnight service at the village church. Old Nianya had stopped in to sit awhile beside Sonia's bed, and Kyril had brought his pillow into his sister's room and was lying beside her.

"How much we shall have to eat and to drink for the Easter feast, Nianya!" said Kyril, thinking of the long flower-decked table that was already spread in the dining room below.

"*Da*," said the old woman. "It is good to feast on Easter Day. It is good to have the table well covered with food, so that all who come to the house may eat their fill. Nearly every hut in our village will have an Easter table ready tomorrow."

"But what will the very poor peasants do, Nianyuska?" cried Sonia. "Aunt Olga says there are some that do not even have one bottle of *kvass* to drink, nor one cake to eat on Easter Day. What will they do?"

"*Och*, my dove," sighed the old woman. "Sad it is and true it is that there are people so poor that they cannot make a feast upon Easter Day. It is not right. No, it is not right. But so it is. Now if it were in the old times when the saints walked on the earth, that would not happen. A way would be found, as in the case of Petrusha, the poor peasant, and his marvelous beer."

"What happened to Petrusha, Nianyuska?" Sonia asked, sitting up straight in her bed. The very thought of a story drove the sleep from her eyes. Kyril settled himself more comfortably on his pillow, and the old woman began the tale.

"Well, then, my little ones, in a certain land there lived

a rich peasant, named Yegor. Yegor had money and Yegor had corn—oh, very much corn. All the peasants in the country about came to borrow from him. But Yegor was mean. When he lent them money, they had to pay him great sums in return. When he gave them corn, they had to pay back every grain at the harvest time and give him, besides, a day's work in his fields for every bushel they borrowed.

"Now it happened one year as Easter drew near, all the peasants in the village were brewing their beer for the holiday feast. That is, all but Petrusha. Petrusha was so poor that in the whole village there was none poorer. On Easter Eve he sat with his wife in his small hut, and he thought to himself:

" 'What shall we do? All the good folk will make merry tomorrow. And we shall have nothing, not even a crust of bread for the feast. I might go to Yegor, but he would not trust me. And also, how ever could I pay him back?' Petrusha thought and thought. Then he got up and stood in front of the icon in the corner of his little hut. And he prayed sadly, saying:

" 'O God, forgive me, a sinner. I have no money. Not even a kopeck to buy oil for the lamp in front of Thy icon. No light will burn there on Thy feast day tomorrow.'

"Not long thereafter there came a knock on his door,

and an old, old man stepped into the hut. 'Greetings to you, Master. May I spend the night with you?' the old man said.

" 'Greetings, Old Man,' the peasant replied. 'Stay if you like! But alas, I have nothing to give you to eat.'

" 'Never mind that, Master. I have three pieces of bread with me. Give me only a mug of water, and I shall have quite enough.' And the old man sat down on a wooden bench with his supper of bread and water.

" 'Why art thou so sad, Master?' he asked, looking up at poor Petrusha.

" 'How should I not be sad, Grandfather? God's Easter festival draws near. Tomorrow all the folk in the village will be merry and glad. But here all is empty. A ball could be rolled from one corner to the other of this bare hut.'

" 'Well, Master,' said the old man, 'perhaps I can help you. Go to Yegor, the rich peasant, and borrow a bushel of his malt from him. Then we can at least brew some beer for the feast.'

" 'He will not lend it to me. And besides, it is too late now. How could we brew the beer in one night? The festival takes place tomorrow.'

" 'Do as I bid you,' the old man said firmly. 'Yegor will not refuse you this time. Go to him and ask for a bushel of malt, and tomorrow for dinner we shall have beer to drink such as no one in the village has ever put into his mouth!'

"Petrusha, the poor peasant, went to his rich neighbor and asked for the loan of a bushel of malt. At first Yegor objected, saying that it was too late to brew beer for the feast, but in the end he loaned the peasant the malt he had asked for. Petrusha came home with the sack of malt on his shoulders.

" 'Good!' said the old man. 'You shall have a real feast. Have you a well in your dooryard?'

" 'Oh, yes,' Petrusha answered, wondering, 'we have a well.'

" 'Then we shall brew the beer in your well. Bring the sack and follow me,' he said to the astonished peasant. They went into the yard, straight to the well.

" 'Throw the malt into the well,' said the old man. Petrusha objected. He did not want to throw away the good malt. It was wicked to waste so. But the old man insisted, and the poor peasant shook all of the malt out of the sack and into the well.

" 'Good!' said the old man. He leaned over the edge and shouted down into the well: 'Water in the well, become beer by morning!—Now, good friend, Petrusha,' he cried to the peasant, 'let us go in and lay ourselves down to sleep. Morning is always wiser than evening. You shall see! Tomorrow for dinner the beer will be ready, and it will be so strong that one glass will be enough.'

"Well, when morning had come and it was time for dinner, the old man said to his host:

" 'Now, Master, get ready all the buckets you can. Place them about your well and fill them up to the brim. Then call in every neighbor to taste your good beer.' The peasant ran from one house to the other, borrowing buckets.

" 'Why do you want all these buckets?' the neighbors asked curiously.

" 'For my beer,' was the reply. And the neighbors wondered how it could be that a man so poor as Petrusha should brew so much beer.

"About twenty buckets Petrusha gathered from among his neighbors. He began to fill them with beer which he dipped up from the well. Such good beer it was! Never had beer like it been tasted or told of. Only in fairy tales does one hear of such a good drink.

"Petrusha, the poor peasant, called aloud to his neighbors, bidding them come to drink his good beer. The people came and they marveled. To see a man pouring water from his well into buckets and then calling to them to drink his good beer! It sounded much like a trick. But when they tasted the beer, they licked their lips in delight. Oh, wasn't it good! 'Never in our lives have we drunk such a drink,' they declared, one and all. And Petrusha, the poor peasant, was glad that he could give so much to his friends.

"Yegor, the rich man, heard of Petrusha's wonderful beer. He begged the poor peasant to teach him the trick.

" 'There is no trick,' said Petrusha. 'You loaned me a bushel of malt. I poured it into my well. And in one single night it has turned into beer. That is all there is to it.'

" 'Well, well, I shall do the same as soon as I go home,' said greedy Yegor. And he gave orders to his servants to throw the very best malt in his barn into his well. The servants hurried to obey. Ten sacks of malt they threw down the well. But the next morning when Yegor went out to taste his beer, the water was still water. The only change was that it had become cloudy.

" 'I did not put in enough malt,' Yegor said to himself. So he ordered his servants to throw in five sacks more. But it was no good. The malt was just wasted. Meanwhile, in the well of poor Petrusha there was clear pure water again. It was as if there had never been beer drawn up from it."

"Who was the old man, Nianya?" Sonia asked, curiously.

"That I do not know," the old woman said. "But he must have been a very good saint. And he came once again

later on to visit Petrusha. One winter's day he knocked at
the peasant's door.

"'Greetings, Master,' he said, 'have you sown grain this
year?'

"'No, Grandfather,' said Petrusha. 'I have been far too
poor. Not a seed have I sown.'

"'Well, then, go to Yegor, the rich peasant, and ask
him for a bushel of each kind of grain that grows. We
shall go into your field and sow it today.'

"'How can we sow the grain now?' Petrusha objected.
"It is winter time, and ice covers the ground.'

" 'Do as I bid you,' the old man commanded. 'Did I not brew beer for you in your well? Well, I will sow grain for you too.'

"Petrusha went to Yegor and borrowed a bushel of each kind of grain that grows. And the old man went with him out to his field, and they strewed the grain far and wide on the ice and snow.

" 'Now,' said the old man, 'go home and wait beside the stove. When summer comes, you shall have bread in plenty.'

"The other peasants in the village laughed at Petrusha. To think of sowing grain in the winter! Everyone knew that grain should be sown in the autumn.

"Well, spring came at last. It grew warm. The snow melted. 'I'll go out and look at my field, anyhow,' thought poor Petrusha. He did not expect to see a spear of grain, but lo and behold, his field was covered with a thick green carpet, such as would gladden the heart of any peasant. The fields of his neighbors who had sown in the autumn were not half so fine as that of poor Petrusha.

" 'Glory to God!' he cried. 'Now I shall be able to better myself.'

"Harvest time arrived. The good folk began to cut their grain. And Petrusha and his wife were busy from dawn until dark, cutting and cutting. They could not possibly cut it all by their own hands. They had to call in their neighbors and promise them part of the grain in return for their help in the harvest.

"When Petrusha, the poor peasant, had cut his whole crop, he knew that now his days of starvation were over. Whenever he needed a tool for his farm, he could take a bushel of grain and sell it in the town. With the money he could buy anything he wanted. And his debt to Yegor, the stingy rich peasant, he paid off in full.

"Yegor was greedy. 'I must sow my grain in the winter, too,' he said to himself. 'Then I shall have crops even finer than that of Petrusha.' So he did not sow his grain the next autumn. He waited till winter. On the very same date on which Petrusha had sown his grain with the old man, Yegor went out to his fields. On his sledge there were many sacks of each kind of grain. He strewed them over his fields to the right and to the left.

"But that very night there came up a blizzard. The snow fell. The wind blew away all his grain and carried it into the fields of his poorer neighbors. Spring came around. The snow melted And the rich peasant went out eagerly to look at his fields. But they were all bare and brown. Not a sprout was to be seen. He could not understand it. For the fields of his neighbors were covered with such thick carpets of green that they were a pleasure to look upon. Then, indeed, did Yegor, the stingy rich peasant, begin to reflect.

" 'How much have I spent upon seeds, all for naught!' he said to himself. 'And those who owe me money and grain have not plowed their land nor sown as much seed; yet their crops are growing. It must be God's will. I suppose it is because I am such a great sinner.' "

The Sweet-Stringed Dulcimer

THE great country house where Kyril and Sonia lived was gay with bright lights and music. The children's parents were giving a fine dinner party to celebrate their recent return from their winter's visit in St. Petersburg. Their friends from the neighboring estates had all been invited, and from their playroom window Kyril and Sonia had watched the sleighs dash up to the door behind the flying horses. It was late in April, but in this northern land snow still covered the ground.

Gypsies had been brought all the way from the city of Moscow to sing and play for the guests. From posts at the head of the stairway, the two children could hear the soft songs and the sweet music of the balalaikas* in the drawing room below. Mademoiselle and Miss had ordered them back to their beds many times. But the children were naughty. They would not obey. At last in despair the governesses had called old Nianya to their aid.

"Come to bed, my little pigeons," Nianya said coaxingly.

"We want to hear the sweet music, Nianyuska," Kyril said stubbornly.

"But it is late, my doves," the old woman protested. "And you will take cold. Come to your rooms, and I will tell you a tale of music sweeter than this and of the enchanted dulcimer* from which it came."

"The words worked as if by magic. The children scurried back to their apartment and soon were wrapped in warm quilts, listening to old Nianya telling the tale of Feodor, the Tsar's son and his enchanted dulcimer.

"Far, far away," Nianya began, "beyond the blue sea, in a vast kingdom, there reigned a Tsar and the Tsarina, his wife. Their names I knew once, but I have forgotten them.

"To the delight of the Tsar and the Tsarina there were born to them two little daughters, the Princess Priceless and the Princess Invaluable. The Tsar was happy with

*Musical stringed instrument.

them. He played with them all the day long, and he thought of nothing but how he should take care of them.

"The little princesses ate from gold plates with golden spoons. They were put to bed on couches of down, and they were covered with furs. The hot sun was not allowed in their tower. No cold breeze blew upon them. And to guard them, the Tsar set seventy-seven maids and seventy-seven menservants.

"One day he heard a great noise in the garden. The maidservants were weeping. The nurses were sobbing. The menservants cried out. For alas, the two little princesses, like Anastasia of the Golden Hair, had been carried off by a great Whirlwind. The Tsar burst into a rage.

"'How now! Seventy-seven maids and seventy-seven menservants could not guard two small princesses? I will riddle them all with arrows at the gates of the city!' he cried in his wrath.

"And the Tsar fell ill with grief. He did not eat. He did not sleep. He only wept and wailed the day through. But the life of man, my little ones, is like a printed cloth; its border has red flowers as well as black and one day to the Tsar and Tsarina there was born a son whom they called Feodor. The child grew and grew; and soon he became a fine figure of a young man. Only one thing troubled the Tsar. Prince Feodor was handsome and sturdy, but alas, there was nothing of the warrior about him. He would handle neither lance nor sword. He would not go to war nor feast with the generals.

"The sole pleasure of Feodor Son-of-the-Tsar was his musical instrument, the sweet-stringed dulcimer. And he played this so well that all who listened forgot everything. If the air was a sad one, a deaf person would weep. If it was gay, a cripple would dance.

"It is a fine thing to make music, my doves, but it does not protect a kingdom nor drive off an enemy. So the Tsar called Feodor to him one day, and he said to the lad:

" 'My well-beloved son, you are strong. You are handsome. I am well content with you. But you are not a brave warrior as you should be. I grow older each year. What shall we do later when foes come to our land? Who will protect your mother and me, if you do not learn how to fight?'

" 'Ah, Lord Tsar,' replied Feodor, 'not always by the sword are cities taken. Not always by blows is the victory won. Often a ruse will serve better than steel. I beg you to test my strength and my vigor! I have heard tell that before I was born my two sisters were carried away by the Whirlwind. Call together your knights, and your warriors and your generals! Send them forth with their swords and their arrows and troops! If one brings back my sisters, let him take my kingdom, and I will become his scullery lad. If none succeeds, I will go forth, and then we shall see whether a good brain is not often more sharp than the sharpest sword.'

"It was done. But among all the generals, the knights, and the brave warriors, none dared to go forth to rescue the princesses from the great Whirlwind. Feodor stepped forth alone to receive the Tsar's blessing.

"And when the Tsar would have given him gold, silver, and gems and great troops of soldiery, the young Prince refused. 'I have nothing to do with gold, silver, or lances,' he said to his father. 'I shall take with me only my sweet-stringed dulcimer.'

"So the brave Feodor set forth to search for his sisters. Where should he go? He walked and he walked, more or less far, by mountains and valleys. One can tell a tale quickly, my children, but not so fast does one act. Each night the ground was his bed and the sky was his coverlid, and each day he went forth over the land.

"At last Feodor arrived at a thick forest. He stopped to listen, for strange noises came out of the wood. On he went among the trees, with fear in his heart. And what did he see, my doves? Two forest giants were fighting and fighting. One hit the other with a great oak tree, and the other struck back with a tall pine. Feodor began to play soft music upon his sweet-stringed dulcimer. The forest giants ceased their battle and began to dance and to sing. At last, worn out, they fell down upon the green earth.

" 'Why do ye fight?' Feodor inquired. 'Ye are forest spirits, not men!'

" 'How should we not fight?' cried one of the giants. 'Along the road we found a treasure. He said, "It is mine;" and I said, "It is mine." We tried to divide it, but that could not be done.'

" 'What is the treasure?' asked Feodor.

" 'A magic cloth, a magic cap, and a pair of magic boots,' was the reply. 'Are you hungry? Spread the cloth, and food and drink appear. Must you go to a far place? Put on the boots, and you take seven leagues in one single step. Does danger approach? Don the cap, and you are not seen; even a dog cannot smell you out.'

" 'I will divide the treasure for you if you wish,' Fedya said to the giants. 'Here, run down the path, and the one who passes the other shall have the cloth, the boots, and the cap.'

"The giants started off. Feodor saw only their heels, so fast did they run into the forest. And for some reason or other they never came back! So Feodor put on the magic cap and the boots, and he carried the cloth away over his arm. Great steps he took in the magic boots, and he soon left the forest far far behind.

"Feodor walked and walked through cities and prairies. At last he came to a crossroads where there was a tiny hut that turned round and round on chicken legs.

" 'Little Hut, Little Hut, turn your face toward me and your back to the forest,' Feodor commanded. And he entered the hut and found there a Baba Yaga with skinny legs and a long nose.

" '*Pfui!*' said the old woman. 'Here comes a Russian. What do you want, my good young man?'

" 'First give me food,' Feodor replied, 'then I will tell you.' The old woman jumped up and heated the frying pan and fed the young man.

" 'I seek my sisters, the Princess Priceless and the Princess Invaluable,' said the Tsar's son. 'Pray tell me, Little Mother, where I may find them.'

" 'I know where you may find the Princess Priceless,' said the Baba Yaga. 'She lives in a white palace in the woods with the King of the Forest. But the road thither is long and hard, and even if you arrive, the King of the Forest surely will eat you.'

"Feodor went on his way. At last he came to the white palace of the King of the Forest. As he tried to climb up

its walls, his foot touched a cord that set many bells ringing. His sister, the Princess Priceless, stepped out on her
balcony; and when she found that it was her brother, she
cried out in dismay:

" 'Alas, my dear brother, Feodor Son-of-the-Tsar where
shall I hide you, that the King of the Forest shall not see
you when he returns?'

"As they were talking, there came a great gust of wind
and the whole palace trembled. Feodor quickly put on the
magic cap which he had got from the two forest giants.

" 'Who rang the bells?' roared the King of the Forest.
'I smell a Russian.'

" 'It may have been a swallow,' the frightened Princess
replied.

" 'No swallow indeed! It is a Russian! I am hungry. I
would gladly eat the low fellow,' the Forest King roared.

"Then Feodor took off the magic cap and bowed low
before him.

" 'Why eat me, O King, when I can give you such a
feast as you never have had since you were born?' he said
to the monster. And he spread out the enchanted cloth.
There appeared twelve menservants and twelve maidservants, who served the King of the Forest with a great
meal. He ate and he ate until he could eat no more. Then
he fell into a deep sleep.

"Feodor learned from the Princess Priceless where their sister, the Princess Invaluable, was held captive.

" 'You must go to her across the waves, for she lives under the ocean with the King of the Sea,' she said. 'The road is long and the road is hard, O Feodor, my brother, and when you arrive the King of the Sea will surely devour you!'

"But Feodor set forth. He went on and on. And at last he arrived at the shores of the broad ocean. There he found some fishermen who took him over the waves in their small fishing boat. A great storm came up. The thunder rolled and the waves rose mountain high. The fishermen trembled at the terrible anger of the King of the Sea.

"Feodor offered to give himself up as a sacrifice. Taking with him his magic cap, his boots, and his cloth, and not forgetting his sweet-stringed dulcimer, he dropped down, down into the sea. The waves became calmer. On and on Feodor dropped, as straight as a key. He landed just beside the palace of the Sea King, where he found his dear sister sitting at the side of the monster.

"The Sea King was hungry. He wished to begin at once to eat up the Tsar's son. But the youth took out his dulcimer and played a plaintive air softly upon it. At the very first note the Sea King grew calm. He sighed great sighs like the bellows down in our blacksmith's shop.

"Then Feodor began to play a gay tune. The Sea King rose from his place. He started to dance. He snapped his fingers merrily, and he winked his eyes slyly. All the fish in the sea swam up to watch. They laughed and they laughed as the Sea King danced on until he could no longer stand on his feet.

" 'What a fine young man! It would be a pity to eat him,' said the Sea King. 'Stay, Son-of-the-Tsar; you shall be my guest. Here, herring and pike, here, you perch and trout, come, serve the table! Bring food and drink for our guest!' So the Sea King and the Princess and Feodor Son-of-the-Tsar all sat down to the feast. The whale danced before them; the herring sang in chorus, and the other fish played on all sorts of instruments. After the dinner, the sea-monster slept.

" 'Tell me, my sister,' said Feodor to the Princess, 'how can I save you and our sister, who lives with the King of the Forest?'

" 'There is but one hope,' the Princess replied. 'Far behind the ocean there is a realm ruled by a Tsarina called the Maiden Tsar. She only can save us, for she alone is feared by the King of the Forest and the King of the Sea. If you but can get into her garden, you may persuade her to help us. But alas, no one is allowed to land on her shores. Cannons guard the entrance. All about the garden is a hedge of tall lances; and on each lance point is the head of a young man who has tried in vain to woo the Maiden Tsar.'

" 'Well, that is indeed something to tremble at,' Feodor replied. 'Terrible is the thunder, but grand is the pity and mercy of God! Tell me the way to the Maiden Tsar's Kingdom.'

" 'I will give you my favorite sturgeon,' said the Princess. 'Upon his back you shall ride, and before you shall go my servant, the sterlet, to show you the way.'

"So Feodor rode forth upon the great fish. and the sterlet

swam on ahead. The little shrimps saluted as they passed by and drove the small fish out of their way.

"At the bottom of the sea, it is not as on the land. There are no ruts nor bumps. The way is smooth as butter. As they slid along, Feodor put on his magic cap so that no one could see him.

"He landed right under the eyes of the guards, who were busy sharpening their swords. And he stepped into the garden, where he walked about and ate apples as if he were the owner. He waited until he saw coming towards him the Maiden Tsar in the midst of her beautiful companions.

"'It is hot. Let us bathe,' said the Maiden Tsar to her ladies-in-waiting. 'Here no eye can see. My guards are so strong that a fly cannot pass them.'

"'A fly cannot pass! But here one has alighted,' said Feodor, doffing his cap and bending low before the Maiden Tsar. The Maiden Tsar jumped back.

"'Do not fear, O Maiden Tsar,' Feodor cried out. 'I would not take you against your will. But if there is in this garden a bride intended for me by Fate, then I wait gladly.'

"The words and the manner of Feodor so pleased the Maiden Tsar that she took him for her bridegroom. Their wedding feast lasted three days and three nights. Then

Feodor asked his bride to tell him how he could deliver his sisters from their captors, the King of the Forest and the King of the Sea.

" 'My beloved Feodor,' said the Maiden Tsar, 'what would I not do for thee! I will send a perch to the Sea King and command him to set free the Princess Invaluable, and I will dispatch straightway a sparrow to tell the King of the Forest to release the Princess Priceless.'

"Feodor sent home with his sisters a message to his father, the Tsar. 'My lord Father,' he wrote, 'you see, one does not arrive always by force. My sweet-stringed dulcimer has proved a far better weapon than a lance or a sword. Come and see us, Little Father! A rich feast awaits you. Later we shall visit you and my two beloved sisters. I wish you long life and good health.'

"Feodor lived long. He governed with justice and entertained his guests so well that they have made this story about him."

The
Bad Wife

I WON'T!" said Sonia crossly.

"Please, Sonia," begged Kyril. "Please come and play with me."

"I won't!" the little girl said again with a scowl.

"Then don't. I'll go and find Kolya," said her brother, running out of the door. Sonia only scowled the harder and turned to look out of the window. Old Nianya, who had come into the room while Kyril was pleading with her, shook her head sadly.

"*Na, na,* Little Sonia, why do you act so?" the old woman said. "Where is our smiling Sonia? All the day long you have been out of temper. That will not do. No one will love a bad-tempered girl. Trouble will come, that

I can tell you. Sit here beside me and listen to the story of the Bad Wife and her sad fate. It all happened because she was so disagreeable.

"A certain man once married a wife whose disposition was so bad that there was no living with her. She paid not the slightest attention to what he said to her. If he asked her to rise early, she would lie in bed for three days. If he begged her to rest, she would rise up to sweep. When he said that he'd like a pancake for supper, she would cry out, 'You idiot, you do not deserve a pancake.' And if he said, "Don't make pancakes today, wife,' she would make a great bowlful and say, 'Eat now, you idiot, until they are all gone.'

"The poor man was worried. He did not know what to do. He went to his wife's parents and asked for the reason for her disagreeable ways. When he learnt that her nurses had all been German and French, he thought to himself.

" '*Nu*, that must be it. She has not learnt Russian ways. Perhaps she was not even swaddled when she was a baby, nor swung in a *liulka*,* like other good Russian children. We must begin again at the very beginning.'

"So he went home and wrapped his wife in swaddling clothes. He put her in a hammock the shape of a *liulka*. And he swung her to and fro just like a small baby. The

*A Russian cradle.

wife was angry at first. She kicked and she screamed. But she could not get out. And she soon became as gentle and kind as when the man had first married her.

" 'At last she is cured,' her husband thought to himself. He was delighted with the success of his scheme. But his delight did not last. For, one day, he said to her:

" 'Now wife, I feel sorry for you. The day is hot. Do not go out into the field to cut hay.' But the Bad Wife made answer in her old hateful fashion, saying: g:

" 'No, no, you idiot! I shall do as I please, and do you follow after me.' And she cut hay all day under the hot sun. The good man knew thus that his wife was not cured.

"The next day he went out into the forest to look for ripe berries. He found a fine currant thicket in the middle of which there was a deep pit. As he stood looking down in it, a thought came into his mind.

" 'Why should I live with a disagreeable wife,' he said to himself. 'I shall put my wife in that pit and teach her a good lesson.'

"The next morning when he rose from his sleep, he said to the woman:

" 'Wife, I pray you, do not go into the forest to pick berries, today.'

" 'I shall go, you idiot,' was the Bad Wife's reply.

" 'Well, don't pick my berries in the fine currant thicket

that I found yesterday in the midst of the forest,' the husband said.

" 'That is just what I will do,' his wife cried, delighted
at doing the opposite of what she was told. 'I shall pick
every bush clean, and I shall keep all the berries for my
own self.'

"The husband went out, and the Bad Wife ran after
him. They came to the currant thicket, and the woman
rushed on ahead.

" 'Don't you dare come near,' the Bad Wife cried out,
as she jumped into the bushes. Then plop! she fell down
into the pit. The man left her there and went back to his
home. For three days he lived in quiet and peace. On the
fourth day he went out into the forest to see how things
were going with the Bad Wife down in the deep pit.

"He let down a rope to pull his wife up, but when he
drew it out again, there, clinging to it, he found a little
Imp. The man was frightened. He was about to throw the
creature back again into the pit, when the Imp shrieked
aloud.

" 'Master, don't put me back there. Don't put me back!
Let me go forth into the free world. A Bad Wife has come
there. She torments us to death. She pinches and bites us.
We are nearly dead with her tricks. Let me stay out and

I will do you a good turn.' So the man let the Imp go free in our holy Russia.

"As they walked along together, the Imp said to the man, 'Master, let us go on to the town of Vologda. I shall enter into the people so that they shall seem to be crazy. Then you shall come along and pretend to cure them. I will go away from them and we shall get lots of money.'

"Well, the Imp and the man went on to the city. Wherever there was the wife or the daughter of a rich merchant, the Imp would enter into her and she would appear to be mad. As soon as the man would come to the house to cure the rich woman, out would go the Imp. Then there would be a feast of rejoicing and a blessing on the house. Everyone thought the man a great doctor. They gave him much money, and they set rich foods before him. He grew very rich.

"At last one day the Imp came to the man. 'You are rich now, Master,' he said. 'You have more than enough. You should be satisfied now. Tomorrow I enter the rich *boyar's** daughter and there I wish to stay. Mind you do not come curing her. If you do, I shall eat you.'

"Well, as the Imp had foretold, the *boyar's* daughter fell ill. She went so roaring mad that she even wanted to devour her own little sister. The *boyar* sent for the won-

*Noble's.

There, clinging to it, he found a little imp.

derful 'doctor' of whose fame he had heard. Now the man feared the Imp. But he had thought out a way by which he might outwit him.

" 'I will cure your daughter, Master,' he said to the *boyar*. 'But you must assemble in front of your door all the townspeople. You must gather together all the carriages and all the coachmen in all the city. The coachmen must crack their whips, and when I give the word, they must all cry aloud, 'The Bad Wife has come! The Bad Wife has come!' Do not fail to do as I say, or my cure will not work. Then the 'doctor' went in to drive out the Imp from the *boyar's* mad daughter.

" 'Why have you come here, O foolish man?' the Imp screamed in rage. 'Did I not tell you I meant to remain? Go away before I eat you!' But the 'doctor' did not go away. Instead he said to the Imp in soft, gentle tones:

" 'What do you mean, O Imp? I have not come to drive you away, if you wish to stay. I came instead to do you a good turn. I came to tell you that the Bad Wife is on her way here, in case you should wish to get out of her way.'

"The Imp rushed to the window, and the man gave the signal to the crowds in the street. Straightway all the coachmen began to crack their whips and to shout:

" 'The Bad Wife has come! The Bad Wife has come! O people, beware, the Bad Wife has come!'

" 'O Master, O Master, where shall I hide?' cried the Imp in dismay.

" 'Run back to your pit,' the crafty 'doctor' replied. 'She will surely not want to go there again.' So the Imp rushed out to the forest and the currant thicket, and he jumped down again into the deep hole.

"Of course, my little pigeon, the Bad Wife was still there. To this day she sits there in the deep pit, along with the Imp. That is her punishment for her disagreeable temper. As for the man, when the Imp was gone out from the *boyar's* daughter, her father's joy knew no end, and he gave the wonderful 'doctor' half of all he possessed."

Rivers
that
Talked

SPRING had come again to the broad countryside. The snow still lay in patches on the brown earth, but it was melting more and more every day. The last icicles on the corner of the huge white country house were dripping themselves away in the April sunshine. The paths across the courtyard to the stables and cottages were no longer stiff with ice and frost, but sank under the feet of the children as they walked beside their old nurse, Nianya.

On the trees near the house the brown buds were swelling and swelling. Some of the bushes had already begun to send forth tiny points of green, and the blue sky overhead was flecked with filmy white clouds. Yesterday a swallow flew past the window of the children's playroom,

and last night Sonia thought she heard a nightingale singing down by the pool below the garden.

The great river Volga not far away was swirling and tossing the huge ice cakes about. Old Foka, who had just returned from a journey to another estate, found the small rivers and streams along the road rushing and roaring, their brown waters risen to the tops of their banks.

"*Da,* my doves," Nianya said, "at last spring is here. The rivers are rising to throw off their white coverlids. They are bursting their ice prisons. Vazuza has waked her sister, the Volga, from her long winter sleep."

"Why is it the Vazuza that wakes up the Volga, Nianya?" Kyril asked curiously.

"It all goes back to the time when the rivers were people," the old woman said, smiling down at the boy. "In the days long ago, the old people say, the rivers were men and women; they could talk with one another as I am talking to you. Well, the river Volga and the river Vazuza were sisters. And like some sisters, my doves, they were always at odds with one another.

" 'I am the cleverest,' Volga would say.

" 'No, I am the cleverest,' Vasuza would reply.

" 'Well, I am the strongest,' Volga would say next. Again Vazuza would cry out that this was not so. All day and for many days the two sisters quarreled. Neither would give in to the other. They quarreled and quarreled. Then one day Volga said to Vazuza:

" 'I have thought of a way to settle the matter. Let us lie down to sleep, Vazuza, my sister. When we awake, let us set forth on our journey down to the sea. She who arrives first will be proven the strongest, the cleverest, and the one who deserves the most honor.'

"Vazuza agreed. The sisters lay down to sleep. But in the middle of the night Vazuza arose without waking her sister. And she started forth on her way down to the sea. 'What is it,' she thought, 'that goes the most swiftly through the broad land? A river, of course!' So she changed herself into a stream and flowed on and on through forest and valley. She chose a short cut and took the straight road.

"When Volga awoke and saw that her sister was gone, she too hurried forth for her journey down to the sea. And she too changed herself into a river. She flowed on and on, neither too slow nor too fast, but just as a great river should flow. At last she caught up with her sister, and she looked at her with such a threatening air that Vazuza grew frightened.

"'Ah, Little Volga,' she said, 'do not be angry. I will agree that you are the strongest and cleverest and the one to whom the greatest honor should be done. Take me in your arms and carry me along with you down to the sea.' So it was done. The Vazuza flows into the Volga and is lost in its waters. But my children, it is still Vazuza who wakes first every year in the springtime and who rouses her sister, Volga, from her long winter nap."

"Could the rivers really talk, Nianya?" Sonia asked, wondering.

"That I do not know, my treasure," Nianya replied. "We say we are wise, but our old folks do not think so. They declare that they are wiser than we. And it was my old father who told me this tale of the rivers that talked with one another. From him I had also the story of the river Volga and her brother and sister, the rivers Dnieper and Dvina."

"Tell us that one, please, Nianyuska," Sonia begged. "Let us walk down the road a bit—the sun feels so warm." The little girl danced along beside her old nurse. The sun was indeed warm, but the air was still crisp and cold, and the children had on their winter fur coats. Old Nianya was wearing a jacket of sheepskin, and over her head was tied her usual kerchief of bright red and blue cotton.

"Well, the river Volga was once a fine young girl, so my old father said," Nianya continued. "The Dnieper River was her brother, and the Dvina, her sister. While they were still children, both their father and mother were taken in death. And the children were left all alone to feed and care for themselves. Not a crust of bread did they eat that they did not earn with their own little hands.

"A tale is soon told, but not so quickly do things happen, my dears. The time went on, and the three children grew up. But no luck did they have. Work, work, work, from morning till night! That was their lot! And what did they get for it? Naught but poor crusts, hardly enough to keep life in their bodies. And as for their clothes, they were just what God put into their way.

"Sometimes they found rags, and with these they tried

to cover themselves. But they were always cold, and they were always hungry.

"One day they had been toiling hard in the grain field since early morn. They sat themselves down under a bush and began to devour their last morsel of bread.

" 'What shall we do, O my brother and sister?' Volga said, weeping. 'How shall we get our food and clothing? How shall we live?'

" 'There is no food for us here,' said Dnieper.

" 'And we have not even rags to shut out the cold!' Dvina exclaimed.

" 'Let us set forth over the world, and when we find a good land, let us turn ourselves into rivers and flow hither and yon in search of good luck,' Volga suggested.

"It was done. The brother and sisters set out together. They walked and they walked. They walked not for one year nor for two years. It was all of three years before they found just the places they wanted. At last they chose the spots where they would start out as rivers to flow over the land. But before they began, they decided to spend the night in a swamp.

"Now, the two sisters were more clever than Dnieper, their brother. No sooner was he asleep than they arose ever so quietly. They chose the best and the most sloping places to start from. They stamped their feet on the ground and changed themselves into rivers. And they began to flow along on their way in search of good luck.

"Well, the brother awoke early next morning. To his surprise there was not a trace of his sisters. He was angry, and he hastened forth to pursue them. He stamped on the ground and behold, he, too, turned into a swift-flowing stream.

"Through the valleys and forests, through the steep rocky ravines, Dnieper rushed on and on. The farther he went, the more angry and fierce he became. But he did not find his sisters. Little by little, as he drew nearer the end of his journey his anger grew less. His waters were calmed, and at last he disappeared into the Black Sea.

"His two sisters, Volga and Dvina, had been running away from him all the time. They flowed swiftly on in two different directions, and at last they, too, hid themselves in the seas. I do not know whether they ever saw each other again, nor what they said. But that the brother was angry at his sisters' deception, that I do know. Anyone can see how fierce he was as he rushed on and on, for to this very day, the river Dnieper flows in a torrent, eating its way between steep banks of earth. The Dnieper flows far faster and with far more rapids and waterfalls than his sisters, the Dvina and our Little Mother Volga."

The children were silent for a moment, their round blue

eyes filled with wonder at these marvelous days of the past. Then Kyril spoke.

" 'Tell us the tale of our own Chorny Ruchei, Nian-yuska," he begged.

This Chorny Ruchei, or Black Brook, was a small river that flowed through a part of Kyril's father's estate. The children often went to it to bathe on warm July days, and their father liked to fish in its waters for the shining brook trout. Farther on in its course the Chorny Ruchei emptied its waters into a blue lake.

"Well, our Chorny Ruchei has a tale all its own," Nianya said, thoughtfully. "Long, long ago, long before even my old grandfather could remember, a man one day set up a mill on the banks of our little Chorny Ruchei. The huge mill wheel churned up the waters, and the little fish who lived in the Black Brook were greatly disturbed.

" 'O Black Brook,' they said, 'save us. Long years have we lived in peace in your waters, happy and free. And now this wicked man has come with his mill to take our water away from us.'

" 'Do not be disturbed, O Fish,' said the Black Brook. 'I will gladly help you.'

"The next day one of the men from a near-by town sat on the bank of the Chorny Ruchei, angling for fish. Suddenly a stranger, dressed all in black, came out of the woods and spoke to him thus.

"'O Fisherman, wouldst thou know of a place where the fish swarm by the thousands? Do me a service and I will show it to thee.'

"'Well, what service is it you wish of me?' the fisherman asked.

"'It is this, O Fisherman,' said the black stranger. 'Go into the town. There thou wilt meet a tall, sturdy peasant dressed in a blue caftan,* in full trousers of blue, and a high hat as blue as the waters of our lake. Say to him: "Uncle Lake, the Chorny has sent me to thee as his messenger. A mill has been set up on his banks, right in his way. He seeks thy aid. As thou shalt decide, so shall it be."'

"The fisherman promised to carry out this service for the stranger in black. And in return the black stranger showed him a place where indeed the fish swarmed by the thousands. The fisherman took from the water that day more fish than he could possibly carry.

"In the town the fisherman met the tall, sturdy peasant in blue caftan, blue trousers, and high hat as blue as the water of the lake; and he faithfully gave him the black stranger's message.

*A long belted coat.

" 'Salute the Brook Chorny,' the blue-clad peasant replied, 'and say to him that, as for the mill, there was not one before; there shall not be one now.'

"The fisherman delivered this message also. And lo, during the night the Brook Chorny rose. Upon the blue lake the waves grew higher and higher. A tempest played havoc over the land. The raging waters swept the mill away during the night, and never again were the fish in the Chorny Ruchei disturbed by a mill wheel."

Nikita appeared and the princess gave him her gold ring.

"Are you warm, maiden?" the frost king asked.

So they shot, each one an arrow in a different direction.

The Tsar listened to their tale.

At last she found herself standing before a tiny hut.

"Swim in the form of a little white duck,
O princess Tatyana."

"And that little taper, what is that for?" Ilya cried.

He rode a red horse with trappings of red.

Kassian
and
Nicholas

"H" SONIA squealed.

"We're stuck!" Kyril cried out in great excitement.

"*Och*, these roads, these roads!" old Nianya exclaimed, shaking her head and leaning far out of the low carriage to see the great mud hole that had half swallowed the wheels.

The children were riding with old Foka, the coachman, in a little low carriage drawn by two horses. The French Mademoiselle and the English Miss were kept at home this afternoon for some reason or other, and so Nianya had been sent out with Kyril and Sonia for their afternoon ride.

The melting snow and heavy rains had made the roads

soft and muddy. Here and there deep pools of water stood in the way; and now the carriage was caught in one as tightly as though in a steel trap.

The horses tugged and strained at their task. Old Foka flapped the reins and cried out to them, calling them pet names and urging them to pull the carriage out of the mud. But it was all of no use. The horses and carriage were stuck fast in the mire. Foka climbed down from his high driver's seat. He picked his way carefully through the mud holes and started off for the nearest village to fetch help.

Kyril and Sonia laughed. They were used to such accidents. In the spring and in the autumn when these dirt roads were so muddy they rarely went out to drive that some such thing did not happen.

"*Och*, if only the good Saint Nicholas would but come along," Nianya said, rubbing her wrinkled cheek with her hand.

"What would he do, Nianya?" Kyril asked.

"Why, he would pull us out of the mire as he pulled out the poor peasant. That's what he would do," the old woman said, shaking her head wisely.

"What peasant?" Sonia asked, and "Tell us about it, Nianyuska," Kyril added quickly.

"Well, it was a day such as this," Nianya said. "Perhaps it was spring. Perhaps it was autumn. I do not know. But the roads were like this one, all mud and mire. A peasant was driving along in a wooden cart. The cart was a poor thing, for he himself had hewn it out of trees cut down in the forest. But it was all he had. He went bumping and splashing through the muddy ruts of the soft road. He drove with the greatest care over the log bridges, for he feared his wheels would slip off and tip his cart into the water.

"At last the poor peasant came to a mud hole deeper than all the rest. It may have been at this very spot in which we are stuck. Who can say? It was long, long ago, before we can remember. It might well have been here. But stuck he was. He pushed and he pulled. He cried out to his old horse. But the cart would not budge. Sometimes he thought he almost had it out, but the wheels would slip back again into the mire.

"The poor peasant was sitting beside the highway, sorry and sad, when along came a traveler. It was Saint Kassian, on his way back to Paradise after a journey upon the earth. But of course the poor peasant did not know this.

" 'Help me, dear friend,' he called to Saint Kassian. 'I am stuck with my cart here in the mire. I cannot get out unless you will aid me. Together we can easily lift the cart out of this great hole.'

" 'Get thee out of my road, peasant,' Saint Kassian replied coldly. 'I am on my way back to Paradise. Dost thou think I shall soil my boots and my caftan to pull thee out of the mud? I have no time to bother myself with such folk as thee." And Saint Kassian went on, leaving the poor peasant sadder than before.

"The man sat mournfully beside his cart. Now and again he would rise and call to his horse. He would push and he would pull, but the cart would not budge. The wheels seemed only to sink deeper and deeper into the mire.

"Then there came another traveler walking along the highroad. This time it was good Saint Nicholas, although of course the poor peasant could not know of this, either. Saint Nicholas also was on his way back to Paradise after a journey upon earth.

" 'Help me, Little Father,' the poor peasant wailed as the traveler approached. 'Here I am, stuck with my cart in the mire, and I shall have to stay here forever if you will not come to my aid.'

" 'To be sure, I will help thee,' kind Saint Nicholas replied. And he waded into the mud up to his knees. Together the peasant and the saint put their shoulders to their task, and after some time they succeeded in lifting the cart out of the hole.

"Now, a little while later Saint Kassian and Saint Nich-

olas arrived in Paradise and presented themselves before the good God.

" 'Where have you been, Kassian, and whence have you come?' God asked the Saint. And Kassian replied:

" 'Master, I was on earth. It so happened that I was passing near a peasant whose cart had stuck in the mire. He asked me to help him, calling out to me to pull his cart out of the mud. But that would have spotted my boots and my caftan. How could I enter Paradise again with my clothes so dirty and so covered with mud?'

" 'Well, God said to Saint Nicholas, 'what about you,

Nicholas? Where have you been to have so much dirt on yourself?'

" 'I, too, was on earth, Master,' Saint Nicholas said. 'And I, too, was passing near the poor peasant whose cart was stuck deep in the mire. He cried out for help. I could not go past and leave him there in the mud. So I waded into the hole with him and we pulled his cart out.'

" 'Well done, Nicholas!' said the good God. 'Now, Kassian, you listen to me. You did not help the poor peasant and you shall be punished. It shall henceforth be four years between your fête days. Only once in four years shall Saint Kassian's day be celebrated and prayers offered to you in the churches. But you, my dear Nicholas, you have done well. Because you have helped the poor peasant to pull his cart from the mire, you shall have two fête days every year. Twice each twelve months, the bells shall ring and the people shall go into the churches to send up prayers to you.'

"So it was, my little pigeons! And so it is to this day. Only in leap year is Saint Kassian's day celebrated, while to Saint Nicholas we send up our prayers twice every twelve months.

"And now here comes old Foka with the men from the village. For us they will take the place of good Saint Nicholas, and we shall soon be on our way again."

The
Little
White Duck

ONE day in early summer Kyril and Sonia were picking wild-flowers beside the tiny lake at the foot of the garden. Old Nianya sat near on a bench at the water's edge. The sun shone down upon them from a blue summer sky. The breezes blew gently, and overhead the larks trilled their sweet song.

Near the great white house the lilacs were in bloom, and here and there under the trees were beds of lilies-of-the-valley, nodding their white bells and scenting the air with their perfume. The white world of winter had changed into a land of soft greens. The birch trees were in full leaf. The fruit trees had blossomed and were already covered with leaves. Everything grows quickly in the Russian summer when the sun shines all day and most of the night.

The children had brought their bunches of wildflowers to show to Nianya, and they had seated themselves on the bench beside her to rest for a while.

"Here come some of the ducks," Kyril cried out, pointing to several white waddling figures marching over the grass.

"The mother duck has brought her children to swim," Sonia exclaimed. They watched the little family hop down from the green bank and swim lazily about upon the shining water of the tiny lake.

"Perhaps it is the Princess Tatyana and her three children," Nianya said, smiling at the tiny procession that was making its way towards them over the water.

"How could a duck be a princess, Nianyuska?" Sonia asked, wondering.

"Very easily, my dove, in the days of the *skazki*," the old woman replied. "The fairy tales tell that the Princess Tatyana lived on a lake in the form of a duck for several years. You see, it happened this way:

"A mighty Prince once married a beautiful Princess whose name was Tatyana. Soon after their wedding the Prince had to leave his lovely young bride.

" 'My dear wife,' he said to her, 'I must go forth to fight our enemies. I must leave you alone here in your tower. I pray you, take care. On no account leave your

"Swim in the form of a little white duck,
O princess Tatyana."

chamber until I return! Beware of disobeying! Believe no soft words, and above all do not listen to the advice of strange women!'

"The Princess wept bitterly and promised her husband to do all that he wished.

"Days and days went by. The poor Princess sat always in her tower, sorry and sad. As the Prince had commanded, she did not set foot outside her own chamber. One day as she sat weeping and waiting for her dear Prince to return from the wars, there came to her a little old woman, who walked with a crutch. To look upon she was a kindly soul, and her voice was sweet as she spoke.

" 'Why do you weep, little Princess?' she said to Tatyana. 'Why are you always so sorry and sad? If you would but come out of your tower into God's world, you would not be so downcast. Come, take a few steps out of doors in your green garden.'

" 'No,' said the Princess, 'I must not go out. I must stay here and wait for my Prince in this tower room.' The old woman persisted. She urged and she pleaded, and at last the Princess gave way.

" 'To walk a little in the green garden, surely that is not a sin,' she said to herself. And she followed the old woman into the garden. Alas, she did not know that the old woman was in truth a wicked fairy who was jealous of her because she had married so fine and handsome a prince.

"So they walked in the green garden, and they came to a little lake whose waters were shining and clear.

" 'How hot is the day!' the old woman said softly. 'How the sun burns, my dove! The water is clear and cool. Let us refresh ourselves in the lake.'

" 'Oh, no, Little Mother,' the Princess said quickly, 'I must not do that.' But she thought to herself, 'To bathe in the lake is not such a great sin!' And she took off her robe and jumped into the water. Hardly had she begun to splash about, when the old woman touched her upon the back, saying, 'Swim in the form of a little white duck, O Princess Tatyana. Only your Prince will be able to free you from the spell I place upon you!'

"The wicked fairy then turned herself into a princess and put on the gown which Tatyana had thrown off. She went back to the tower and sat down in the poor Princess's place to wait for the Prince to come home from the wars.

"At the first bark of the dogs and at the first tinkle of the bells on the harness of the horses, she rushed forth from the tower and threw her arms about the neck of Tatyana's husband. So glad was the Prince to reach home again that he did not perceive that this fairy was not his own true wife.

"Down on the lake the poor Princess Tatyana swam around and around in the form of a white duck. In her nest on the bank she laid three smooth round eggs, and later these hatched out three little ducklings. She raised them with care. She taught them to catch the tiny gold fish that swam in the lake, and she gathered bits of rags to make them three little coats.

"One morning the ducklings jumped out of the water and began to walk about on the green grass of the lawn.

" 'Do not go there, my children!' the white duck cried out. 'A wicked fairy lives near. She has destroyed me, and she will do you harm also.'

"But alas, her children were like all children, my little pigeons. They would not heed their mother's advice. One day it was a game in the grass on the bank of the lake. The next day it was a more daring excursion across the green lawn. Always a little bit farther! Always a little longer were they gone. And at last they waddled right into the court of the palace itself.

"The wicked fairy knew them at once. She ground her teeth in her anger, but she made no outward sign. She called the ducklings to her with honeyed words. She gave them food and fresh water and she made them lie down to rest in a comfortable chamber. Then she went out into the courtyard and had her servants build up a great fire of logs. She ordered them to hang the kettles above it and to sharpen their knives.

"In the little chamber two of the ducklings soon fell fast asleep. But the third was afraid, and he did not close his eyes. He only listened. The wicked fairy came to the door of the chamber and called out softly, 'Are you asleep, my little dears?'

" 'We sleep without sleeping,' the wide-awake duckling replied, speaking for his brothers as well as himself. 'We dream that someone wishes to kill us and to cut us in quarters. We see piles of logs and boiling kettles, and we hear the noise of sharpening knives.'

" 'They are not yet asleep,' the fairy said to herself. So she went away. Later she came again to the door. 'Do you sleep, my children?' she called. And again the little duck replied for himself and his brothers.

" 'We sleep without sleeping. We dream of piles of logs and boiling kettles and we hear the grinding noise of sharpening knives.'

" '*Na*,' the wicked woman said to herself, 'always the same words in the same voice. I had best go in and see how this can be.'

"Softly, softly she pushed open the door. She saw two of the ducklings lost in a deep sleep, and she straightway killed all three.

"Next day at dawn the little white duck called to her children. There was no answer. She called and she called. The glade was silent and still. Her heart was sad with foreboding. She spread her white wings and rose into the air. She flew over the palace courtyard, and there on the ground, as white as your handkerchief and as cold as the fish here in our lake, lay the three little ducklings.

"The white duck rushed to them. She spread her wings over them and in a sad piercing voice, she began to lament:

> " '*Quack, quack, my children!*
> " '*Quack, quack, my dears!*
> *You were born in my sorrow*
> *And washed with my tears.*
> *I have watched at your pillow,*
> *I have wept at your bed.*
> *Long have I loved you—*
> *Now, alas, you are dead!*'

"From his window the Prince heard these human words coming from the bill of the white duck. He marveled, and he called his wicked fairy bride to him.

" 'Wife, do you hear this wonderful happening? That white duck speaks with the words of a woman,' he said in astonishment. But the fairy only replied, 'You must have dreamed it.' And she ordered the servants to drive the duck from the courtyard. The servants chased the white duck, but they could not drive her away. Each time she returned once more to her dead children. And from his window the Prince again heard the little white duck speak in these words,

> " 'Quack, quack, my sweet children!
> Quack, quack, my dears!
> The wicked fairy has killed you.
> Alas, for my fears!
> The Prince's bride is a serpent,
> A poisonous snake,
> While she sits on my throne,
> I must dwell in the lake.'

" 'Catch me that white duck,' the Prince ordered his servants. They rushed to obey, but it was in vain. The little white duck flew this way and that, and could not be caught. Then the Prince himself stepped down into the courtyard. And, my little pigeons, the white duck flew down and lighted upon his very shoulder.

"The Prince must have guessed the whole dreadful story. For he took the little white duck gently by her two wings. He held her in front of him and said, 'O White Duck, be-gone! Stand before me as a lovely young princess once more!' And lo, the white duck was gone, and before the

Prince stood his dear Princess Tatyana, as beautiful as when he had left her in her tower.

" 'My husband,' said Tatyana, "while I swam on the water in the form of a duck, I learned many things. Send a servant to the birch tree that grows beside the lake. There he will see the nest of a magpie. And in the magpie's nest he will find two crystal balls. One contains the water of life and the other is filled with the water of speech.'

"All in the courtyard marveled as the servant returned from the birch tree with the two crystal balls. They watched the Princess Tatyana as she sprinkled the little ducklings with the water of life. Behold, they arose, three beautiful boys, alive and well. Their mother then sprinkled them with the water of speech, and they rushed to their father, crying out loving words.

"Thus was the whole family united once more. As for the wicked fairy, I do not know whether she was punished or not. Had I been the Prince, I should have tied her to the tail of a horse and drawn her hither and yon over the country. But the Prince and the Princess did not want to do anything but to enjoy the present and to forget the past."

Marco the Rich
and
Basil the Luckless

N A certain kingdom, in a certain state, there once lived a merchant called Marco the Rich," said Nianya, beginning one of the *skazki* which Kyril and Sonia loved so well to hear. "Marco had treasures without number, but he was stingy and mean. He would send off poor beggars empty-handed from his door, and would order the servants to loose the dogs upon them. Now we all know that beggars are truly the children of God. It is not good, my little pigeons, to turn a beggar away from your house, without even a kopeck* or a crust of dry bread.

*Russian copper coin worth about half a cent.

"Well, on a cold winter night two poor old gray-haired men came to Marco the Rich and asked him for shelter. The old men begged long and hard, and the merchant at last sent them to stay in a hut out in the farm yard where his old aunt lay dying.

"The next morning Marco was struck dumb with wonder when he saw his aunt walking towards him, hearty and strong. 'Why, Aunt,' he cried out, 'yesterday you were at death's very door! Today you are well. What can have happened?'

" 'O Marco the Rich,' the old woman said, 'strange things took place in my hut last night. Two old gray-haired men spent the night there. It may have all been a dream, but it seemed to me that at midnight I heard a knock on the window. And a voice spoke to the two beggars, saying:

" ' "In your village, Little Fathers, a babe has been born. What name will you give him? And what gift will you send?" The old men made answer: "We shall name him Basil the Luckless, and as our gift, we shall promise him all the possessions of Marco the Rich." '

"Marco was angry. He ordered his sleigh and he drove forth to the village to find out if it was true that such a babe had been born. He drove straight to the priest's house.

" 'Indeed, yes, O Marco,' the priest made reply to the rich merchant's question. 'Such a babe was born yesterday, I have given him the name Basil, and have nicknamed him the Luckless, because he was born to such very poor parents. I have not yet christened the child, for I cannot find a godfather for him.'

"Marco the Rich offered himself as the godfather. The priest's wife was the godmother, and the christening feast lasted far into the night. Next day Marco the Rich sent for the babe's father.

" 'My good man, you are poor,' he said to the peasant. 'You will not be able to take proper care of your son. Give him to me and I will bring him up as my own in my fine house; and for you, there will be a gift of one thousand roubles.'* The peasant consented. Marco the Rich wrapped up the baby in soft fox furs, and he drove off with him in his swift three-horse sleigh.

"It was winter. The ground was covered with snow and ice. It was bitterly cold. Well along on the way Marco the Rich had his sleigh stopped. He handed his godson to a servant and said, 'Take the babe by the feet and throw him over that cliff.'

"The servant did as he was bid, and the cruel Marco smiled to himself. 'Now then, Basil the Luckless, there will

*Russian silver coins, each worth about fifty cents.

be a fine chance of your enjoying the possessions of Marco the Rich,' he said under his breath.

"But on the third day after this, a party of merchants happened to pass along the very same road. They were bringing a great sack filled with gold coins to pay the debt they owed to Marco the Rich. Near the cliff they heard the cry of a child, and they stopped to find out what it could mean. Their servant climbed down to the bottom of the cliff and there, to his amazement, he found a lovely green meadow with the child lying upon a bed of sweet-smelling spring flowers. The merchants rushed to see the marvel. Then one gathered the child into his arms and wrapped it up in his own warm fur coat.

"When he heard of the finding of the babe in the green meadow, Marco the Rich guessed at once that the child was Basil the Luckless. He begged the merchants to give the baby to him. He placed before his guests a great feast, and he offered to forgive them their debt if he could but have the child. So the merchants consented.

"One day went by. Another day passed. And on the third day Marco the Rich put the baby, Basil the Luckless, into a barrel. He smeared the barrel with tar and threw it into the sea. The barrel floated and floated. It sailed over the water to the walls of a monastery, far, far away from the home of Marco the Rich.

"A monk, who had come out to fetch some water, heard the child's cry inside the barrel. He set forth in a boat, rescued the barrel, and knocked off its hoops. Lo and behold! there was the child. The monk took the baby into the monastery, and the good abbot also gave him the name of Basil the Luckless.

"For eighteen years Basil lived with the monks. They taught him his letters, how to read and to write, and how to sing in the choir of their little chapel. The good abbot loved the boy well and made him the keeper of his vestry.

"Now, my doves, it so happened that Marco the Rich

was traveling abroad collecting the money that was owing to him. One day he came to the monastery where Basil was living. And during his stay he learned the strange history of the young vestry keeper. Marco the Rich knew at once that the lad was none other than his godson, and he begged the abbot to let him take the boy home with him.

"At first the abbot refused, but when Marco the Rich offered to make a great gift of gold to the monastery, the good man consented. Then the wicked merchant sent his godson off home bearing a letter to his wife, which read thus:

" 'Wife, send the bearer at once to the soap factory and order the workmen to push him off into the great boiling kettle. Take care! Mind that you carry out my order exactly! The youth is my enemy.'

"Basil the Luckless trudged over the roads toward the house of his godfather. Along the way he met up with an old gray-haired man, who greeted him kindly and asked where he was going.

" 'I am bearing a letter from Marco the Rich to his wife at home,' said Basil the Luckless.

" 'Show it to me, O good young man,' the old grandfather asked. And when he had read the letter. he handed it to the lad. Tears rolled down the cheeks of Basil the Luckless, as he read of his doom, but the old man comforted him saying, 'Do not grieve, my young master. God will not forsake you.'

"The old man blew upon the letter, and lo, the seal was whole as before. 'Now go on your way! God speed you!' he said. 'And do not fail to give this letter to the wife of Marco the Rich! Have no fear! No harm will befall you!'

"When the wife of the rich merchant had read the letter, she called to her daughter, Anastasia. She showed her the letter, and much to the wonder of Basil the Luckless, the girl read aloud thus: 'Wife, the bearer of this letter is the bridegroom I have chosen for our dear daughter, Anastasia. Wed them at once! Do not delay! Be sure to do as I order! It is my will.'

"Now, when people are rich, they need neither to brew nor to bake. All is ready. So the feast was held the very next day, and the marriage took place. Basil was fine in new caftan and boots,
new caftan and boots, and he pleased Anastasia. They were wedded at church, and everyone ate, drank, and made merry.

"The following day Marco the Rich returned to his home. When he saw Basil the Luckless, he flew into a rage. 'How dared you wed our daughter to him?' he roared at his wife. 'It was by your order,' she cried, as she showed him the letter written in his own hand.

"The wicked merchant was still determined to make an

end of poor Basil. So when three months had passed, he spoke to him thus:

" 'Go forth, through the twenty-seven kingdoms and the thirtieth empire, to the land of the Serpent Tsar. Collect from him all my debts, and find out what has become of my twelve lost ships.'

"Early at dawn Basil the Luckless set forth on his errand. He said his prayers before the holy icon, bade farewell to his wife, and filled his knapsack with dried crusts of bread. Did he walk a long time or a short time? Was it near or was it far? I do not know, but suddenly he heard a voice, saying:

" 'Basil the Luckless, where are you going?'

" 'Who calls me?' asked Basil, for he saw no one at all.

" 'It is I, the Wise Oak,' the voice replied.

" 'I am going to the Serpent Tsar to collect debts for Marco the Rich,' Basil said to the Wise Oak.

" 'Well, when the time comes, think of me,' said the Oak. 'I have stood here for three hundred years. Find out from the Serpent Tsar how much longer I must stand.'

"Basil consented, and he went on and on. He walked and he walked. At last he came to a wide river and entered the ferryboat. The Ferryman also wanted to know where he was going, and he, too, asked the youth to find out from the Serpent Tsar how long he must toil back and forth over the river.

" 'I will not forget you,' Basil promised the Ferryman, and he went on his way. He walked and he walked, and at last he arrived on the shore of the blue sea. A Whale Fish was lying there. His great body was stretched from one shore to the other, and people were walking over his back as though he were a bridge. As soon as Basil had set foot upon him, the Whale Fish spoke to him.

" 'O Basil the Luckless, where are you going?' he asked. And when the young man told him of his errand, the Whale Fish cried out, 'Oh, when the time comes, do not forget me. Here I lie forever and ever across the blue sea. People walk and ride over me all the day long. They have worn the very flesh off my bones! How long must I lie here?'

" 'All right,' said Basil, 'I will not forget to find out.' And he went on and on until he came to the palace of the Serpent Tsar. What a fine palace it was! What beautiful rooms! And in the most beautiful of all, Basil the Luckless came upon a maiden who sat alone on a couch.

" 'Who are you, my good young man?' the maiden said to the youth.

" 'I am Basil the Luckless, come to collect the debts of Marco the Rich from the Serpent Tsar.'

" 'Not to collect debts are you sent here,' the maiden declared, 'but that the Serpent Tsar might devour you. How have you come? What have you heard along your way?'

"Basil the Luckless told the maiden of the Wise Oak, of the Ferryman, and the Whale Fish. He had just finished his tale when a great storm arose. The palace rocked with thunder, and the earth shook beneath it. The maiden hastened to hide Basil under the couch, and then the Serpent Tsar flew into the room.

" 'I smell a Russian,' he roared.

" 'How can there be a Russian smell here?' the maiden replied. 'You must have been flying over Russia yourself. You have brought the smell with you.'

" 'Well, I am tired,' the Serpent Tsar said. 'Come, comb my hair for me!' The maiden obeyed, and while she ran the comb slowly through his thick hair, she said to the Serpent,

" 'O Tsar, I have had a strange dream today. I thought I saw a great Wise Oak that cried out to me, 'Ask the Serpent Tsar how long I must stand here!' Now, what could that mean?'

"And the Serpent Tsar answered, 'That Oak must stand there until a gallant young man kicks it in the direction of the rising sun. Then only will the Wise Oak fall. And in its roots will be more gold and silver than in all the treasury of Marco the Rich.'

" 'Then I dreamed, O Serpent Tsar, that I met a Ferryman, who had been pushing a ferryboat across the wide river for full thirty years. He, too, asked me how long he should have to continue to ferry people across from one side to another.'

" 'Not long,' said the Serpent Tsar. 'Let him put his first passenger into his place and push the ferry away from the landing. Then the passenger will become the Ferryman and he it will be who shall ferry people across the river forever.'

" ' I had still a third dream,' said the maiden as she combed the hair of the Tsar. 'I was walking across the back of a Whale Fish that spoke to me, asking how long he should have to serve as a bridge over the sea.'

" 'You should have told him to throw up the twelve ships of Marco the Rich, which he carries inside him. Then he would sink under the water. Flesh would cover his bones. And he would regain his former strength.'

"When the beautiful maiden let Basil the Luckless out of his hiding place, she gave him a bit of good advice. 'Take care, Basil the Luckless,' she said to the youth, 'that you tell what you have heard here only when you are safe on the other side of the waters.'

"Basil thanked the young maiden and turned his face

homeward. He walked and he walked; and at last he came to the blue sea. The Whale Fish asked if he had spoken of him to the Serpent Tsar, and Basil the Luckless told him how he should be delivered, but he told it only when he had reached the other side of the sea.

"The Whale Fish hiccupped mightily. Lo and behold, from his great mouth the twelve lost ships of Marco the Rich floated out with full sails! The whale straightway sank under the waves, and the sea rose so high that Basil the Luckless found himself standing in water up to his knees.

"Later on, Basil met again the poor Ferryman. 'Did you speak of me to the Serpent Tsar?' the Ferryman asked.

" 'Yes, I did,' Basil answered, 'and as soon as you have ferried me over the river I will tell you how you may deliver yourself.' When he had jumped out on the bank, Basil called back to the man, 'Give your place to your first passenger, push the boat away from the landing, and go to your home.'

"Last of all, the young man came once more to the Wise Oak. He himself kicked it in the direction of the rising sun. The Oak Tree fell down, and there in its roots lay a great treasure of silver and gold. Basil turned round, and behind him, just sailing into the harbor, came the twelve lost ships of Marco the Rich. The sailors loaded the silver and gold from the roots of the Wise Oak onto the ships; and then they set sail with Basil on board.

"When Marco heard that his son-in-law was sailing home with his twelve ships, and that the Serpent Tsar had given him greater treasure than his, he grew pale with anger. He ordered his sleigh and set forth himself to the kingdom of the Serpent Tsar. He was determined to find out a way to get rid of the youth.

"Marco came to the ferry and sat down in the boat. The Ferryman put the merchant in his own place and pushed the ferry off over the water just as Basil the Luckless had told him to do. And from that day to this, my doves, the wicked merchant has had to ferry the people from one side to the other of that wide river.

"Basil the Luckless came home to his wife and his mother-in-law. He helped the poor, and gave gifts to the beggars and orphans. He gained more and more wealth, and he enjoyed all the possessions of Marco the Rich just as the two old gray-haired beggars had foretold."

The
Water King's
Daughter

UPPER was over. The children had finished and had risen with the others from the long table in the dining room. They had stopped at the door to kiss their mother's hand, as was their custom after each meal. Then they had gone upstairs to their playroom and had stepped out on the little balcony to sniff the soft summer breeze.

How sweet the air smelled! The scent of the cut hay on the prairies was strong on the warm wind. All day the peasants had been working out in the fields, for the harvest had begun. In the great house everyone had been busy from morning until night. Old Nianya had not left the side of her mistress throughout the long day. Together they had looked over the stores. They had directed the work in the great kitchen, in the dairy, and in the vegetable rooms where peasant girls were busy drying the vegetables and fruits for sale and for home use in the winter to come.

"*Och*, my doves," said the old woman, coming out on the balcony, "I am weary tonight. From early morn we have worked, but at last evening brings rest. Tell me of your doings on this bright summer day."

"We spent the afternoon beside the Black Brook, Nianyuska," Sonia said. "We fished and we bathed. There is a splendid pool in the brook that is just right for swimming."

"*Nu*, you must take care, my dears. You must not swim too far, or the King of the Waters will pull you down into his underground realm."

"Tell us a *skazka* about the King of the Waters," Kyril said to Nianya.

"Tell us a new one, Nianyuska," Sonia begged.

"Well, let me see," their old nurse said thoughtfully. "Perhaps I have not yet told you of the beautiful Natasha, the Water King's daughter, and how she delivered Nikita Son-of-the-Tsar."

The children pulled their chairs closer to the old woman. They, too, were tired with their long day's play, and they leaned their heads against her as she unfolded another of her wonderful tales.

"Far beyond the twenty-seven prairies, in the thirtieth empire," Nianya began in her usual fashion, "there lived a Tsar and his Tsarina. One time the Tsar was abroad upon a long journey, and during his absence the Tsarina gave birth to a beautiful boy, who was called Nikita Son-of-the-Tsar.

"It was a summer day just like this, and the Tsar was on his way back to his own kingdom. The sun blazed down upon him. The heat was intense. The Tsar grew so thirsty that he stopped for a drink at the edge of a lake which he was passing just then. He lay down on the bank and drank long draughts of the icy water. Suddenly he felt a tug at his beard, and behold, the King of the Waters had him fast in his grip.

" 'Let me go,' cried the Tsar.

" 'I will not,' the King of the Waters replied. 'How dare you to drink here without my permission?'

" 'Let me go,' said the Tsar. 'Ask me what you will, only let me go home.'

" 'Well,' said the Water King, 'there is that in your palace of which you know nothing. Give it to me and I will release you.'

"The Tsar thought to himself, 'How can there be in my

place any thing of which I know nothing?' And so he gave his promise and went on his way.

"As he neared home, the Tsarina came running to meet him with the little Nikita Son-of-the-Tsar held out in her arms. To her surprise the Tsar burst into tears at the sight of the babe. And she, too, wept when he told her of his promise to the King of the Waters, for they both knew that the thing of which the Tsar had known nothing must be his baby son.

"But tears do not mend anything, my little pigeons. The Tsar's son grew and grew, and at last the time came when his father dared no longer forget his promise to the Water King. So he led his son down to the lake where he had drunk on his way home from his journey.

" 'Search here for my ring, my son,' the Tsar said to the youth. 'I lost it but yesterday.' And he went away, leaving his son by the water. As the lad looked for the ring, there came to him a tiny old woman, who greeted him, saying, 'What are you doing, O Nikita Son-of-the-Tsar?'

" 'Go along with you, Mother, leave me in peace,' Nikita said crossly, not even looking up from his search for the ring.

" 'Peace be with you. God guard you,' the old woman said, turning away. Nikita was troubled. 'Why should I speak so to that kind old woman?' he thought. 'I had best call her back.' He ran after her, asking her pardon for his impolite words. And he told her of his search for the ring his father had lost. The old woman shook her head.

" 'Not to find a lost ring were you sent here, O Nikita Son-of-the-Tsar,' the old woman declared. 'Your father has given you to the King of the Waters. He will come for you soon and take you with him into his watery land.' The youth burst into tears, but the old woman comforted him, saying:

" 'Do not weep, Nikita! For you there shall be days of joy as well as days of sorrow. Hide yourself in these currant bushes! There will fly down to earth twelve snowy white doves who will turn into twelve beautiful maids. Then will come a thirteenth, the most beautiful of all. While they bathe in the lake, you must make off with the blouse of the last comer. Only return it when she gives you her golden ring.'

"It all happened just as the old woman had told. The thirteenth maid was of a beauty such as never was seen save in a *skazka*. When she found her blouse gone, she cried out in these words:

" 'Whoever you are that has hidden my blouse, come forth! If you are an old man, I will be as your daughter. If you are a young man, you shall be my dear friend.'

Nikita appeared, and the Princess gave him her gold ring in exchange for her blouse.

" 'Nikita Son-of-the-Tsar,' she cried to the youth, 'why have you been so long in coming? The King of the Waters is angry. I will point out the way to his watery kingdom. Go along boldly! You will meet me there also, for I am his daughter, Natasha the Fairy!'

"Natasha changed herself again into a dove and flew quickly away, while Nikita followed the road to the watery kingdom. There he found fields, prairies, and bowers, just as upon earth. The sun shone upon him as it shines down upon us. The King of the Waters greeted him with reproaches for his delay.

" 'This shall be your punishment, Nikita Son-of-the-Tsar,' the Water King declared. 'Behold these vast plains, with their ruts, pits, and rocks! By tomorrow this land must be smooth as my hand. The rye must be growing, tall enough that a crow may hide itself in it. If not, you shall pay for your fault with your life.'

"Poor Nikita wept bitterly in his despair. The beautiful Natasha saw him from her tower and asked him why he was so sad.

" 'How shall I not weep when misfortune arrives?' the poor Prince replied. 'Your father, the Water King, demands that I level all these rocky plains in one single night, and that tomorrow the rye be found growing upon them, tall enough that a crow may hide itself in it.'

" 'That is no misfortune,' Natasha replied. 'Go to sleep and God guard you! Morning is wiser than evening. Do not worry, Nikita! All will be ready.'

"Nikita slept soundly. Meanwhile Natasha went out on her tower balcony and called her fairy servants to her. 'Go, fill up the pits,' she commanded. 'Take out the rocks. Sow the rye, that all may be ready before the sunrise.'

"When Nikita awoke, all was indeed ready. Before his eyes was a level plain as smooth as your hand and covered with a rich harvest of rye, tall enough so that a crow might hide itself in it.

" 'Well done, Nikita Son-of-the-Tsar!' the Water King said when he saw the smooth green prairie. 'Now I will give you a second task. Here are three hundred ricks of ripe grain, each one of which has three hundred bundles. Thresh it all for me! And see to it that you do not disturb even one of the ricks or untie one of the bundles. If it is not ready by sunrise, you shall pay with your head.'

"Again Nikita crossed the courtyard in tears, and again the Fairy Natasha asked him why he was so sad.

" 'How shall I not be sad? Misfortune has come to me,' the Tsar's son made reply. 'The King of the Waters has ordered me to thresh three hundred ricks of three hundred bundles of ripe wheat. I may not disturb one of the ricks or untie a single bundle of grain. And all must be ready before the sunrise.'

" 'Here is no misfortune. That will come later,' Natasha said to the Prince. 'Go to sleep! Do not fret! Morning is wiser than evening. All will be ready.'

"When the Prince was asleep, the Water King's daughter stepped forth on her balcony and called out in a loud voice: '*Hola!* You creeping ants! Every ant under God's sun, run to me now! I have work for you. Take out, before sunrise, each grain of wheat in the ricks of my father!'

"In the morning the Water King asked Nikita Son-of-the-Tsar if his task was done. They went out to the threshing floor, and behold, my little dears, each rick was in place, no bundle untied. And in the granary all the sacks were filled to overflowing with grain.

" 'Well done, Nikita Son-of-the-Tsar!' the Water King said. 'Now for your third and last task of all. I bid you to build for me, before the sunrise, a church of pure wax.

"For the third time Nikita crossed the courtyard in tears, and a third time the Fairy Natasha comforted him, saying, 'All will be ready.'

"On her balcony the Water Princess called out, '*Hola!* All you bees that fly over the fields under the sun, fly hither to me! I have work for you. Build me a church of purest wax, and see that it be ready before the sunrise.'

"In the morning Nikita showed the Water King a great church built all of pure wax. What a beauty it was, with its domes and its crosses! The King of the Waters was delighted with it.

" 'Never has any young man served me so well before,' he said to Nikita. 'I am well pleased with you. I will make you my heir and you shall choose your bride from among my thirteen beautiful daughters.'

"Nikita chose Natasha the Fairy, and soon they were wed. There was a wedding feast that lasted three days, and Nikita dwelt with his bride in her high tower room in the watery kingdom."

Three Golden Hairs

"DID Nikita ever go home from the watery kingdom?" Kyril demanded, as the old woman paused.

"*Nu*, that is another *skazka*, my treasure," Nianya replied. "It is now growing late, and we shall be scolded if you are not soon in your beds."

"But the sun is still so bright, we could not sleep! Only one more story, dear little Nianya," Sonia replied eagerly. The old woman patted the little girl's head. Bedtime had come, but the child was right, the sun still shone brightly on this "white night" of summer when the dark never came to this northern land.

"Well, just this one tale," the old nurse said, giving in as she usually did to the little girl's pleading. "You see, Nikita Son-of-the-Tsar dwelt a long time in the watery kingdom. At first he was happy, but by and by he grew homesick, and he longed to return to his own holy Russia. One day his fairy wife, Una, found him in tears at their tower window.

" 'Why do you weep, dear Nikita?' she asked.

" 'I long to see my mother and my father,' the Tsar's son replied. 'I long to go back to my home in holy Russia.'

" 'Now at last here is misfortune indeed!' Natasha said, sadly. 'We dare not go away. The Water King would be angry. He would pursue us and kill us. But if you are set upon going, we must think up a plan for our escape.'

"The Water Princess pulled three golden hairs from her head. She placed each one in a different corner of their tower room. Then she fled away quickly with Nikita towards holy Russia.

"Early next morning there came to the door the servant whose duty it was to wake the young couple. He knocked and cried out, 'Wake, Prince and Princess! You have dreamed long enough. The King bids you come to him!'

"In reply, one of the three golden hairs spoke up in the voice of Natasha the Fairy,

" 'It is too early,' said the hair. 'Go away! We have not

slept long enough yet. Come back in an hour.' So the servant went away. An hour later he knocked again on the door of the tower room.

" 'The time for sleep is over,' he called out. 'The time for rising is come.' And the second golden hair cried out in the voice of the Princess, saying: 'Wait but a little. We are rising. We are dressing ourselves. Come back in an hour.' So the servant went away.

" 'The King of the Waters is angry,' the servant said when he returned at the end of an hour. 'He bids you come to him at once.' This time the third hair cried out, 'Tell the King of the Waters that we shall be there in a minute.' The servant waited and waited. Then he knocked once again. This time there was no answer, and when they broke the door open, they found the tower room empty.

"Well, wasn't the King of the Waters cross then! He sent out a troop of soldiers to catch the young couple, who were by this time far, far away, galloping, galloping over the prairies.

" 'Get down and lay your ear to the ground, Nikita Son-of-the-Tsar,' Natasha said to her husband. 'Listen well and tell me if we are pursued.'

" 'I hear the voices of men and the feet of their horses,' Nikita replied. 'They are drawing nearer and nearer!' Natasha the Fairy quickly changed their horses into a green field. She turned Nikita into an old shepherd and herself into a white sheep. Then the soldiers rode up.

" 'Well, old man,' they said to the shepherd. 'Have you seen a young prince and a beautiful maiden?'

" 'No, my good folk,' the shepherd replied. 'I have not seen anything. For forty years I have been tending my sheep here on the green prairie, and not a bird has flown over me, not an animal has run past.' So the troops turned around and went back to the Water King.

"Well, the King of the Waters flew into a fine rage when they told him their story. 'Why did you not arrest them?' he cried to the soldiers. 'Those were my daughter and the son of the Tsar.' And he sent out another troop of soldiers to catch them.

" 'Come, Nikita, climb down from your horse and put your ear to the ground,' said Natasha the Fairy, as they rode along. 'Listen well and tell me if you hear anything!'

" 'I hear the voices of men and the stamping of horses' feet,' Nikita replied.

" 'They are coming!' cried Natasha. "We must be quick.' And she changed herself into a church and Nikita into an old priest, while the horses became two tall green trees. The soldiers galloped up, and they halted at the sight of the old priest and the church under the trees.

" 'Ah, Little Father,' they cried, 'have you seen an old shepherd tending a sheep in a green field?'

" 'No, my good people,' the old priest replied. 'I have not seen anything. Here for forty years I have served in this church and not a bird has flown over me, not an animal has run past.' So the troops turned around and went back to the Water King.

" 'Lord, we have seen nothing but an old priest and his church under the trees. No trace could we find of either shepherd or sheep.'

" 'Idiots!' the King cried out in great anger. 'You

should have torn down the church and captured the priest. Those were the Prince and my daughter, Natasha. I will send no more soldiers. I will go forth myself.' The Water King set out on the swiftest steed in his stable, galloping, galloping like the north wind, always in pursuit of Natasha and Nikita, who were far, far away.

" 'Put your ear to the ground, Nikita Son-of-the-Tsar, and tell me whether you hear anything,' Natasha said to her husband for the third time.

" 'I hear the voice of a man and the hoofbeats of a horse, only this time they are louder,' Nikita replied from his post on the ground.

" 'Alas, it is the King of the Waters himself,' cried Natasha the Fairy. 'We must be quick.' She changed the horses into a lake. She turned Nikita into a drake and herself took the form of a little white duck.

"The King of the Waters galloped swiftly up to the edge of the lake. He knew at once that the drake and the duck were Nikita and Natasha, and he straightway turned himself into an eagle.

"The eagle swooped down upon the drake and the duck. It tried its best to kill them. But all in vain! As soon as the eagle flew down to attack, the duck and the drake plunged into the water. Again and again the eagle swooped down upon them. But it was of no use. At last he gave up the fight! He turned himself again into the King of the Waters, mounted his horse, and rode off again to his watery kingdom.

"Nikita and Natasha rode along on their way. Was it long? Was it short? I do not know, but at last they came to a wood in the Tsar's kingdom in the thirtieth empire.

" 'Wait for me here, wife,' Nikita said to his bride. 'I will ride on ahead and announce our arrival to my father and mother.'

" 'Alas, Nikita Son-of-the-Tsar, you will forget me,' the Water Princess said sadly.

" 'Never will I forget you,' Nikita declared.

" 'Do not swear it, O Tsar's son, for indeed it will be as though I did not exist. Only promise to think of me when you see two white doves beating their wings on the window panes of your chamber.'

"Nikita gave Natasha his promise and rode off alone to the palace. In his joy at returning, he did indeed forget the fairy bride whom he had left in the wood. He lived one day. Then another! Many other days passed. And he gave never a thought to poor Natasha alone out in the forest.

"Poor Natasha waited and waited in the little wood. At last she made her way into the royal city. She engaged herself as a cook in a bakery, and one day she took two pieces of dough and shaped them into two doves.

" 'You could not guess what these two bits of dough will become,' she said to the baker, as she put them into the oven.

" 'Of course, I can guess,' the baker replied. 'They will become loaves of bread and we shall eat them. What else could they become?'

" 'Wait and see,' Natasha said. She opened the oven and threw back the window. The pastry doves trembled. They spread their white wings and flew out of the bakeshop in the direction of the palace.

"Nikita Son-of-the-Tsar was sitting alone in his chamber. Suddenly he heard a noise at the window, and looking up he saw two white doves beating their wings against the clear panes. At first he tried to drive the doves away, but they would not go. Again and again they beat their white wings on the window panes. Then at last, all at once, he remembered the words of his fairy wife and his promise to her.

"The Tsar's son sent messengers out in all directions to search for the daughter of the Water King. They sought her in the woods and in the fields near the city. They sought her through the streets, and at last in the bakery they found her.

"Nikita took her hand eagerly and kissed her sweet lips. Then he led her to the palace and presented her to his mother and father. The Tsar and the Tsarina gave a great feast, and there was food and drink for everyone in the kingdom. I have heard my father tell about it so often that it seems as though I were there and myself had eaten and drunk and made merry with Nikita and his fairy bride."

The Peasant,
the Saint,
and the Prophet

HE July afternoon was warm. The sky was filled with dark clouds, and far to the west thunder was heard now and again. Old Nianya had brought her knitting out into the garden, and the two children had come to sit down beside her on a bench under an apple tree.

"It will surely storm before evening," Nianya said, as a roll of thunder was heard far in the distance. "But then today is the fête of Ilya the Prophet. It always rains on his day."

"Why, Nianya?" asked Kyril. "Why does it always rain on Ilya's fête day?"

"Because he is the saint of the harvest time, my little

pigeon," the old woman explained. "If all the peasants do not make a good feast for Ilya, he is apt to grow angry. Then he sends thunder and lightning and even hail on their crops. It is to please him that the farmers tie bundles of oats and rye upon their gates. And that he may bless the harvest, the priest holds a service in the church to honor him. It is not good to anger Ilya, as you shall see by the tale that I am going to tell you."

"A long, long time ago there once lived a peasant. On the days of Saint Nicholas he always made feasts, but of the fête days of Ilya he took never a thought. Ilya's day came and went, and the peasant did nothing. He would even work in the fields as though the day were the same as the other days of the year. When Saint Nicholas's day came he would go to the church and offer a candle and take part in the service. But for the Prophet Ilya, he never lighted even the very smallest of tapers.

"Now it happened one morning that the Prophet Ilya and Saint Nicholas were walking upon earth. They came to the land that belonged to the peasant. What fine fields they were! So green and so thick was the grain growing upon them that it did one's heart good.

" 'Here will there be a good harvest, an excellent harvest,' Saint Nicholas said. 'And this peasant deserves it. He is a good fellow. He is honest and pious. He thinks about

God and he remembers the saints. This grain will fall into very good hands.'

" 'We shall see by and by how much grain he will have,' Ilya declared. 'This man needs a lesson. When I have burnt up his land with my lightnings and when I have beaten it flat with my hailstones, then this peasant of yours may remember to keep my day holy, too.'

"Saint Nicholas tried to turn the prophet away from his wicked intention, but all in vain. So he went to the peasant.

" 'Sell all your grain as it stands now, O peasant,' he said. 'Sell it to the priest of the Prophet Ilya. If you don't, you will have nothing, for Ilya means to beat your grain down to the ground with his sharp hailstones.'

"The peasant rushed straightway off to the priest.

" 'Wouldn't you like to buy some fine standing wheat, Little Father?' he asked. 'I'll sell you my whole crop now, for I need money at once. I'll sell it all cheap. When harvest time comes, you shall have every grain.'

"They reached a fair price. The peasant got his money and went along to his hut. Some time later there came rolling up a great storm-cloud. It rained and it hailed. The sharp stones cut down the peasant's grain as though with a knife. Not a blade was left standing.

"The next day the Prophet Ilya and Saint Nicholas came walking by.

" 'Now you can see what a good job I have done in your peasant's grain field,' Ilya said, with a laugh.

" 'The peasant's!' exclaimed Nicholas. 'That grain does not belong to the peasant at all. It belongs to your priest. But indeed you have made a fine job of it.'

" 'The grain belongs to the priest? How can that be?' Ilya asked, wondering.

" 'Why, the peasant sold his grain as it stood to your priest only last week. The priest has already paid him. Now he will have to whistle for his wheat.'

" 'Stop!' Ilya said. 'That must not be! I will set the field right again. The grain shall be twice as thick and twice as good as before!'

"When they had finished their walk, Saint Nicholas hurried around to the hut of the peasant.

" 'Go quickly, O peasant,' he cried, 'and buy back your crop. Do as I bid you! You will lose nothing by it.'

"So the peasant went again to see Ilya's priest. He greeted him politely and said: 'Little Father, I see that God has sent you a great misfortune. The hail has beaten your grain down to the earth. You can roll a ball over the field from one side to another, it is so flat. But I will help you, nevertheless. I will take my field back. Here is half of your money!' And they shook hands on the bargain.

"Meanwhile, goodness knows how, the grain field of the

peasant began to grow green. Up from the ground shot tender new leaves. Rain fell on the fields at just the right moment. The sun shone warm upon it, and the young shoots grew and grew. Up there sprang a fine crop. The heads grew so heavy that the stalks bent down to the ground. The sun turned the grain yellow, and when harvest time came the peasant's fields looked like pure gold. He was just gathering his grain and putting it into tall ricks, when the Prophet Ilya and Saint Nicholas chanced to walk past.

" 'Only look, Nicholas!' cried the prophet, his face beaming with pleasure. 'See what a blessing I have given my priest! Such a reward he will never forget in all his life.'

" 'The priest!' Saint Nicholas exclaimed. 'Why, Brother Ilya, what do you mean? To be sure, such a harvest is indeed a great blessing, but the grain belongs to the peasant. The priest has got nothing whatever to do with it.'

" 'What are you saying?' Ilya asked, puzzled.

" 'What I say is true,' Saint Nicholas answered. 'When the hail beat down the grain, the peasant went to your priest and bought it all back at half of its price.'

" 'Stop!' cried the angry Ilya. 'I shall yet get the best of this peasant who dares to forget my holy days. No matter how many sheaves he shall lay down on his threshing floor, he shall thresh out exactly a peck of grain at a time.'

" '*Nu*,' said Saint Nicholas to himself, 'this is a bad job!' And he hurried away to the hut of the peasant. 'Mind you, peasant,' he said to him, 'when you thresh your grain, put only one sheaf on the floor at a time.'

"The peasant began to thresh out his grain. He obeyed the good saint, and he put only one sheaf on the floor at one time. And the words of the Prophet Ilya came true. From each sheaf of wheat he got a whole peck of grain. His sacks and his bins were soon filled. His storehouses overflowed. He built himself new barns and stored them to the roof.

"Then one day Ilya and Saint Nicholas came walking past. The prophet looked at the new barns in the greatest surprise.

" 'Look, Nicholas, look!' he said to his companion. 'See those new barns! What shall the peasant have to put into them?'

" 'Well,' Saint Nicholas replied, 'they seem to be already full.'

" 'Where ever did that peasant get so much grain?' the prophet demanded.

" 'Bless me, Brother Ilya, you gave it to him yourself,' Saint Nicholas cried. 'You said that he should have exactly one peck of grain each time he threshed. He only put one sheaf on the threshing floor at a time, so of course he got out a peck of grain for each sheaf.'

" 'Ah, Brother Nicholas,' Ilya said, shaking his head. 'Now at last I know the truth. You go and tell the peasant everything that I say.'

" 'What an idea!' Nicholas protested. 'That I should tell everything!'

" 'Well, well, we must not talk about it,' Ilya said to Saint Nicholas, 'but just the same, your peasant shall not get the best of me again.'

" 'What are you going to do now?' Saint Nicholas asked.

" 'Aha, that I won't tell you,' Ilya said firmly.

" 'Here's a bad job, indeed,' Nicholas thought to himself. 'My good peasant is in great danger.' And he set forth, running to seek the peasant again.

" 'Here, peasant,' he cried. 'Listen to me! Go and buy two church tapers, a great one and a small one; and be sure that you do with them just as I tell you.' And he explained to the peasant what he should do with the great and small taper.

"Well, the next day the prophet and the saint were walking along together dressed as two travelers. They met up with the peasant who was carrying in his hands the two wax church tapers. One was a big taper as thick as his wrist, that must have cost a whole rouble, while the other was a poor little taper as thin as a straw, not worth more than a kopeck.

" 'Where are you going, peasant?' Saint Nicholas asked.

" 'Why, I'm on my way to the church,' the peasant replied.

" 'And what shall you do with your wax tapers?' the Prophet Ilya demanded.

" 'Well, I shall light this great taper for Ilya the Prophet. He's been ever so good to me. When my grain was knocked flat by the sharp hailstones, he made himself busy and worked me a miracle. He gave me a fine harvest twice as good as the first that was ruined by hailstones.'

" 'And that little taper, what is that for?' Ilya cried.

" 'That's for Saint Nicholas,' the peasant said as he went along on his way.

" 'There now, Ilya,' said Saint Nicholas. 'Does that look as though I had told of your doings? Surely you can see how much truth there was in that foolish idea of yours.'

"So the tale ends. Ilya was flattered. His anger was calmed. He did no more harm to the peasant's crops. The peasant lived well and his harvests were good. But he had learned his lesson. From that day he took care to make a fine feast each year for the Prophet Ilya, as well as for the good Saint Nicholas."

"And that little taper, what is that for?" Ilya cried.

Elena
the Fair

S TAND still, please, Little Sonia," said Tanya, the sewing woman who was fitting a fancy dress costume upon the little girl. "How shall I have your dress ready in time for the fête, if you wriggle and squirm?"

But it was hard to keep still, Sonia thought, when one had a fine new Russian costume to admire in the mirror. The tall pointed headdress with its pearl beads and paste gems glistened so brightly. She just had to twist about now and then to catch a glimpse of the great green and gold bow that covered the back of her head and the broad silken streamers that fell almost to the hem of her blue satin skirt. Tanya was having great trouble in keeping Sonia still long enough to fit the soft white blouse which she wore under a little jacket of gold cloth.

"*Na, na*, my dove," said old Nianya who had brought her mending into the sewing room. "Stand still for Tanya, and she will make you as fine as the Princess Elena on her throne in the tower. Do not budge for a few minutes, but listen to me! Forget yonder mirror and I will tell you the story of Elena the Fair.

"'Long before my father, or my grandfather, or even his grandfather, was born, there lived in a certain land a Tsar who had a beautiful daughter called Elena the Fair. So lovely was she and so dazzling her garments that the like has never been heard of save in a fairy tale.

"When the time came for the Princess to marry, her father, the Tsar, had built a tall tower set upon twelve mighty columns and twelve sturdy beams. There, on her high throne, awaiting her suitors, sat Elena the Fair, her headdress covered with jewels and her robes of pure silk.

"Now in this same land, my dove, there was a certain man who had three sons. He taught them all reading and writing and the other learning that comes out of books. And he said to them, 'My sons, when I shall die, take care that you each read prayers over my grave!'

"'It shall be done, Little Father,' the three youths declared.

"Well, not long thereafter the old father died. Now the older sons were fine fellows, handsome and strong, while the youngest, Ivan who was called Vanya, was slender and very much weaker than they.

"One day there came word from the Tsar's palace that the Princess Elena would wed any youth who, with one leap of his steed, should reach her in the tower and kiss her on the lips. All the young men in the kingdom were stirred by the thought of this beautiful bride. Vanya's two older brothers talked of nothing else from morning till night. Only Vanya remembered his promise to his dead father.

" 'Brothers,' said he, 'our father lies in his grave. Who of us shall read the prayers above him tonight?'

" 'Whoever wishes to, let him go to the grave,' the older brothers replied curtly, their minds full of the princess. So Vanya went, while the two others stayed at home to dye their mustaches and to practice with their horses the jumps which they thought might help them to win the beautiful Princess.

"A second night came. 'Brothers,' said Vanya, 'I have done my full share of reading the prayers at the grave of our father. It is your turn now. Which of you will go?'

" 'Whoever wishes to go, let him go,' the brothers replied. 'We have other business to do. Go away! Do not bother us!' And they put on their caps. They shouted to their horses, and they rode this way and jumped that way over the broad country. So Vanya read prayers again at the grave of his father. And on the next night as well he went forth alone.

"Next morning the two older brothers groomed their steeds well. They made ready to go to try their luck at the tower of the Tsar's daughter, Elena the Fair. 'Shall we take Vanya with us?' one said to the other. 'No,' said the second. 'The people would only laugh at him. He would disgrace us!' So they rode away, leaving poor Vanya behind.

"Vanya was sad. He wanted so much to have just one look at the beautiful Princess in her tall tower. He wept as he went out to his father's grave in search of comfort. And his father heard his weeping. Suddenly he rose out of his coffin and stood before the young man.

" 'Do not weep, my dear Vanya, I will help you,' he said. The old man drew himself up tall and straight, and called out in a loud ringing voice. He gave a shrill whistle and, from goodness knows where, there came a galloping horse. And such a horse, my treasure! The earth shook under its hoofbeats. Fire spurted from its nostrils and ears, and with mighty leaps it cavorted about the old man and his son. At last it stood still and said, 'Old man, what are thy wishes?'

" 'It is my wish that thou shouldst carry my son to the tower room of Elena, the beautiful Princess, daughter of the Tsar,' the old man said to the horse.

"So Vanya crept into one of the horse's ears and out of the other, and when he set foot on earth again, he turned into a knight so handsome and strong that no words can tell of it. He mounted the horse and, setting his arms akimbo, he flew off like a falcon to the palace of the Tsar.

"All the youths of the land were gathered there in the courtyard. They marveled to see such a fine knight upon such a glorious steed. With a wave of his hand Vanya lifted his horse into a mighty leap to the Princess's tower. A roar went up from the crowd when he almost reached the top. He failed only by the breadth of two beams. Then he turned his steed about and galloped off a short distance. He wheeled, darted forward, and made a second great bound into the air. This time he missed by only the breadth of one beam.

"Once more Vanya turned his horse round about. Once more he wheeled. And once more he galloped up to the tower. Like a flash of swift lightning his steed flew through the air. With a mighty bound he jumped to the very window of the tower chamber. And Vanya leaned over and kissed the sweet lips of the lovely Princess Elena, who thrust into his hand her ring of pure gold.

"Then wasn't there a hubbub down in the courtyard! 'Who is he? Who is he? Where is he? Oh, stop him!' the people cried out. But Vanya had gone. Not a trace of him was to be found. For he had galloped back again to the grave of his father. There he loosed the brave horse and knelt down on the ground.

" 'What shall I do? How shall I act, O Little Father?' he cried. And again the old man rose from his coffin to help the good youth.

"That night when the two brothers returned to their home, they found Vanya asleep up over the stove. They waked him to tell of the wonderful happening at the Tsar's palace.

" 'What a fine knight he was! We should have taken you with us, little brother! Never shall we behold his like again!' they cried to Vanya. But Vanya said nothing.

"The next day there was a great assembly in the court of the Tsar. The palace was filled with nobles and princes, and Vanya's elder brothers were among the crowd in the vast hall. Vanya went, too, but nobody noticed him, for he arrived upon foot and kept himself hidden in a dark corner. Only upon his finger he wore the golden ring which the Princess had given him.

" 'Where is my bridegroom?' the Princess Elena said from her place on the glittering throne. 'Let him come forth!'

"But no bridegroom appeared. She sent forth her servants to seek the brave knight who had jumped up to her tower on the day before. But no such knight could they find.

"You are wondering why Vanya did not step forward, my dove? Well, I will tell you. 'I pleased her before when I came as a knight, riding upon a glorious steed,' the lad said to himself. 'Now let her fall in love with me again in my everyday caftan.' And Vanya waited there in his dark corner, with a smile on his lips.

" 'If my bridegroom will not come forth, I shall seek him myself,' said Elena the Fair. She stepped down from the throne and moved about the great hall. She looked at this one and that one, and her eyes shone so bright that they lighted up the whole chamber. At all the young men she looked, but each time she shook her head. It was not he!

"Then at last she came upon Vanya, sitting so quiet and so modest in his dark corner, with her ring upon his finger. To the wonder of all, she cried, 'Here is my bridegroom!' And she made Vanya take his seat beside her upon her golden throne. The very next day the wedding took place, and how happy they were!

"As for the bridegroom, how clever he turned out, and what a brave handsome fellow! Just to see him mounted upon his glorious steed, with a cap on his head and his arms thrust akimbo, you would say right away that he was a born Tsar. You would never believe that he had once been poor little Vanya."

By the
Pike's
Command

THE kitchen of the country house of Kyril and Sonia smelled strongly of fish, but the children did not notice the odor at all. They were far too interested in the work that was going on all about them. For days the cooks had been busy drying and salting fish that had just been caught in the river Volga, near by.

The kitchen tables were piled high with fish of several kinds. There were herring and bream, sterlet and sturgeon. From the eggs of the huge sturgeon, maids were preparing the delicious caviar which Kyril and Sonia liked so well spread upon toast or upon pancakes.

Nianya was superintending the drying of the fish for

the winter storerooms underground. She knew exactly how the fish should be prepared. She had her eye on each of the peasant girls who had been called in to help with the work. It was near the end of the day. The women were tired, but there was yet much to be done.

"What is this, Nianya?" Kyril asked, pointing to a fish with a long head and a very large mouth.

"That is a pike," Nianya replied. "Now if we hadn't killed it, perhaps it would serve us as the pike served Emilian in the old fairy tale. Then our work would be easy."

"Dear Nianyuska, tell us about the pike and Emilian," Sonia begged, her face beaming with pleasure at the thought of another of Nianya's stories. The peasant girls looked up from their work. Their tired faces brightened, for they, too, liked to hear the old fairy tales.

"Well, we think we know much," Nianya began, "and old people say they know more. But the *skazki* tell us of things that even they do not know. Once, long, long ago, there lived three brothers. Two were sharp-witted, but the third—well, the third, whose name was Emilian, was thought such a stupid that people called him the Fool.

"One day the two clever brothers set forth to take their goods to the markets in the towns down the river. And they said to Emilian:

" 'Now listen, you fool! While we are gone, do you obey

our wives! Treat them with respect as if they were your own mother! And perhaps we will bring you from the towns down the river a red caftan, a red blouse, and a pair of red boots!'

"So saying, the two clever brothers went their way to the markets along the great river. But the Fool shook his head and said to himself: 'I am to pay them respect, am I? Good! I will pay them respect, but in my own way.' And he stretched himself out upon the warm stove and went off to sleep.

" 'Foolish fellow, wake up!' the sisters-in-law cried, nudging Emilian as he lay snug and warm upon the stove. Your brothers have commanded you to obey us, but there you lie on the stove and do not stir yourself. How shall you receive a red caftan, a red blouse, and a pair of red boots, if you do nothing to earn them? Here, take these pails! At least go and fetch us some water for our soup.'

"Emilian the Fool took the two pails and went out to the river. As he scooped up the water, a fish swam into his pail. It was a pike like yonder one over there on the table.

" 'Glory be!' cried the Fool. 'Now I shall have a fine meal. I will cook this pike for my supper and I will eat it myself. My sisters-in-law never give me enough to fill my empty stomach.' Then, to his surprise, the Pike spoke to him in good Russian words.

" 'Don't eat me, Emilian,' it said. 'Put me back into the river, and you will be sure of good luck!'

" 'What sort of good luck can you give me, O Pike?' Emilian demanded.

" 'Why, the best of good luck!' the Pike declared. 'Whatever you wish, that I will do for you. Look, I will show you. Say, for example, "By the Pike's command, Pails, go home and put yourselves in your places!" '

"The foolish youth laughed, but he spoke as the great fish had directed. And lo, the pails immediately went home all by themselves. When Emilian returned, there they were in their places on the bench near the stove.

"The sisters-in-law wondered. They whispered together, saying: 'Emilian may not be so stupid as people think. He is clever enough so that his water pails come home by themselves and set themselves in their places!'

"A little later they called again to the Fool. 'Emilian,' they cried, 'why are you lying there, idle and lazy? Get down from the stove! There is no wood for the fire. Go out in the forest and fetch us some logs!' Emilian climbed down. He took two sharp axes and got into the sledge, but he did not harness the horses.

"The sisters-in-law laughed when they saw that he had forgotten to hitch the horses to the sledge. After all, they said to one another, he was but a stupid fool. They did

"What sort of good luck can you give me,
O Pike?" Emilian demanded.

not hear the youth say to the sledge, 'By the Pike's com-mand, Sledge, drive me into the forest.' But they did see the sledge move off all alone at a rattling pace as if drawn by three galloping horses, and their eyes grew round and wide at the marvel.

"Emilian passed through the town at a terrible pace. The people were pushed out of the road. They grew very angry. They cried out: 'Stop him! Oh, stop him!' But it was all of no use. They could not lay hands on him, so fast did the sledge-without-any-horses fly over the roads. Arrived in the forest, the Fool jumped down from the sledge and seated himself comfortably upon a dry log.

" 'By the Pike's command, O Axes,' he said, 'let one of you cut down the trees! And let the other chop them up into firewood!' In a jiffy the sledge was piled high with wood. Emilian said again, 'By the Pike's command, O Axes, cut a thick club for me!' The words were hardly out of his mouth before a stout club lay up on the top of the sledgeload of wood.

"Now while the Fool had been in the forest, the towns-people had gathered themselves in the road. When he came rattling back on his sledge-without-horses, they stopped him and began to pull him about.

" 'By the Pike's command, O Club!' Emilian cried out in a loud voice, 'get thee up and protect me!'

"Up jumped the club. It thumped the people over the head. It smashed in their ribs. It knocked them down in the road like so many bundles of rye. The Fool got away and sat again on his sledge and rode to his home. When the wood was heaped up, he climbed again upon the stove to take his ease and to sleep.

"*Och*, weren't the townspeople angry with Emilian the Fool! They went to the Tsar and complained of him, saying:

" 'O Little Father, you must do something to help us! This man rushed through our streets on a sledge-without-horses. He thumped us over the head. He knocked us out of the way. He is a clever one. We cannot get hold of him by running about after him. We must set a trap for him. The best way to bring him here will be to promise to give him a red caftan, a red blouse, and a pair of red boots.'

"So the Tsar's messenger came to see Emilian the Fool. 'Go to the Tsar!' he said to the youth who still lay upon the stove. 'He will give you a red caftan, a red blouse, and red boots.'

" 'Well,' said Emilian, 'I am warm here, I do not wish to move. Still I should like well enough to have a red caftan, a red blouse, and a pair of red boots. I will go to the Tsar.'

" 'By the Pike's command, O Stove!' Emilian cried,

without rising, 'take me at once before the Tsar.' The eyes of the messenger started out of his head in amazement as he saw the stove move away with Emilian lying on top. And it was in this fashion, my dears, that Emilian the Fool arrived before the Tsar and his court.

" 'Put him to death!' cried the angry Tsar, when the stove halted before him.

"But the Tsar's daughter who stood close to her father laughed merrily. It delighted her to see a young man arrive in the palace in such a strange manner.

" 'O my father, do not harm him,' the Princess begged earnestly. 'I like this young man. Give him to me for my bridegroom!' The Tsar flew into a rage at the very idea. But the girl begged and pleaded that she might marry Emilian. Each time she spoke, the Tsar grew more angry.

"At last he cried in his rage, 'Very well, foolish girl, you shall marry him, and you shall both be set adrift upon the blue sea!' The wedding was held. Emilian and the Princess were put into a barrel which was smeared over with tar. They were thrown into the sea. Was it a long or a short time that the barrel floated about upon the blue waves? I do not know. But at last the poor Princess could bear it no longer.

" 'O husband,' she cried, 'save me! I shall die! Do something to get us out of the sea and onto the shore!'

" 'By the Pike's command,' cried Emilian, 'O Barrel, cast thyself on the shore and burst thy sides open!' Behold, it was done.

"Emilian and the Princess stepped forth on the seashore. They wandered about, looking for shelter, and at last the Princess begged her bridegroom to build for her some sort of a house.

" 'By the Pike's command,' Emilian cried, 'let a marble palace be built. Let it be placed before the house of the Tsar. And let it be the finest in the whole world.'

"In an instant it was done. The next morning when the Tsar arose from his bed, the first thing he saw was a beautiful palace of purest white marble. He sent forth his messenger to find out whose it could be, and when he learned that his daughter and Emilian were living there, he summoned them to him. He pardoned Emilian and made peace with his daughter. And they all lived together happy and content. Was all this a dream? How should I know! But the old people say it happened, and so we must believe them."

Three Kopecks
and a
Cat

RAIN beat upon the panes of the playroom window. The garden paths were covered with water, and the birch trees at the corner of the low white house dripped and dripped without ceasing. Summer was over. Autumn had come with its rains and chill winds.

A wood fire was burning in the tall porcelain stove in the corner of the playroom. With her chair drawn close to its warmth, Nianya sat sewing, and beside her was Sonia with her gray cat in her lap.

"Give me your cat, Sonia," Kyril said, teasing her. "She is too lazy and sleepy. Let me pull her tail once and I'll wake her up for you."

"You shall do no such thing!" Sonia cried, holding her cat tighter.

"*Nu, nu,* my young falcon," Nianya scolded the boy gently. "Do not tease your sister. You will do well to treat Sonia's cat with respect. Those who are good to the beasts usually get their reward. Come, sit down with us and I will tell you the tale of the orphan lad and the cat who brought him good fortune.

"Well, my little pigeons, there was once a poor orphan lad. His name I have forgotten, but we may call him Mitya. Mitya was poor. He had nothing to live upon. His bread and his clothing he had to earn by his own hand. So he hired himself out to a rich peasant for the wage of one kopeck a year. When the twelve months were past, his master called Mitya to him and put into his hand the kopeck he had promised him.

" 'If I have truly earned this money,' Mitya said to himself, 'I can go forth again into the free world. But I must be sure. I will drop it into the well. If it floats on the water, that shall be a sign that I have served my master faithfully and that I may keep my kopeck.'

"The youth dropped his kopeck into the well, but it did not float. It sank to the well's bottom, and so Mitya went on working for a second year.

"When, at the end of the second twelve months, the

rich peasant put another kopeck into the youth's hand, honest Mitya said again to himself, 'Now if I have truly earned this money, I may keep it and go forth into the free world. But I must make sure. I will drop it also down into the deep well. If it floats, it shall be a sign that I have done my work faithfully and that I may keep my kopeck.' But again the kopeck sank to the bottom of the well.

"At the end of the third year, Mitya's master was pleased with the good lad. He offered to give him a whole rouble as his wage. But Mitya refused, saying, 'I hired to you for a kopeck; a kopeck I will have.'

"So the master put that coin into his hand. Straightway Mitya took his kopeck out to the well and dropped it over the edge. As he bent down to watch it, to his surprise, he saw on top of the water all the three kopecks, floating like leaves. He gathered them up and put them into his pocket, and he set forth again into the free world.

"Into the town he went. He walked through the streets, looking at this thing and that thing. And all at once he came upon some boys teasing a cat, just as Kyril declares he would like to tease your pussy, my little Sonia. Now Mitya was kind-hearted. He could not bear to see anything suffer.

" 'Give me that kitten,' he called to the boys.

" 'We will sell it to you,' they replied.

" 'What do you want for it?' asked Mitya.

" 'Three kopecks,' was the answer. Mitya took out of his pocket the three kopecks he had earned in his service with the rich peasant. He picked the cat up into his arms and went forth again in search of shelter and work. This time he engaged himself to a rich merchant who kept a fine shop. As for his cat, it slept in a corner of the shop by day and caught mice by night.

"From the moment that Mitya and the cat set foot in the shop, the merchant's business improved. All the day long people came to buy at good prices. The merchant could not keep enough goods on his shelves, and soon the purchasers had bought everything he had.

" 'I must go over the seas to buy new goods for my shop,' he said one day to Mitya. 'I have a ship ready. I set sail today. Let me take your cat with me! He will amuse me and he will catch the mice on the ship.'

" 'Take him and welcome,' said the good-hearted Mitya. 'Only if you should sell him, you must pay me his price. I warn you he is not cheap.'

"Well, the merchant set out in his ship. He sailed over the blue sea, and he came to a far land where he put up at a certain inn for the night. Now the keeper of this inn was a rogue. 'This merchant is rich,' he said to himself. 'He must have much money upon him. I will put him in the corner room where the rats can get at him. If they eat him up, then his money is mine.'

"You see, little pigeons, that land was a strange country. They had no cats in the whole kingdom, and the rats and the mice had got the best of everybody.

"The merchant took his cat and went up to his room. He went to bed and to sleep. But the cat stayed awake. The next morning the innkeeper came to his door. He opened it boldly, for he expected to see the poor merchant dead, devoured by rats. To his surprise there was the merchant, alive and well, holding Mitya's cat and stroking its fur. The cat was purring and purring, and on the floor in the corner there was a pile of dead rats, as high as the stove. The innkeeper was struck dumb with astonishment. He had never seen such a thing in all of his days.

"'Master Merchant,' he cried eagerly, 'Sell me that beast.'

"'Gladly,' said the merchant.

"'What do you want for it?' the innkeeper asked.

"'Almost nothing,' said the merchant. 'I will make the beast stand on his hind legs while I hold him by his fore-paws. Then you shall lay up gold pieces around him until he is hidden. I will be content with that small sum as his price.

"The innkeeper agreed. The merchant left the inn with

the sackful of gold which he had got for the cat. When he had finished up his affairs in that strange land, he turned his ship homeward. As he sailed the blue sea, he had plenty of time to think about Mitya, the cat and the gold.

" 'Why should I give so much money to an orphan?' he thought to himself. 'A sackful of gold is too much for a cat. No, much better keep the most of it for myself.'

"But the moment he had made up his mind to this sin, there arose a great storm. The winds tossed the waves high over the ship. The lightning flashed bright, and the thunder roared through the sky. The merchant repented. 'Sinner that I am,' he cried, 'I am about to take what does not belong to me. O Lord, forgive me. I will not keep back from Mitya a single kopeck of the price of his cat.'

"As he prayed so, the wind ceased. The waves became calm, and the ship sailed on and on.

" 'Welcome home, Master. Where is my cat?' Mitya cried out as soon as the merchant had landed.

" 'I sold him,' said the merchant. 'Here is the money, every rouble and kopeck.' Mitya took the sack of gold. He left the merchant and went down to the seashore where the seacaptains were, just returned from far lands. With the gold his cat had brought him, the good lad bought a shipload of finest incense. He spread it out on the sand and set it afire in honor of God. As the blue smoke drifted toward Heaven, a sweet smell spread far and wide over the land. Suddenly Mitya found an old man standing beside him.

" 'Which dost thou prefer, young sir,' said the old man, 'a good wife or great riches?'

" 'I do not know, Old Man,' Mitya replied.

" 'Well, go and find out,' said the grandfather. 'See those three brothers plowing over there in that field? Go, ask their advice!'

"So Mitya went to speak to the peasants who were tilling their land.

" 'God give you aid, Masters,' he said in salute.

" 'Thank you, good lad,' they replied. 'What do you want of us?'

" 'An old man sent me to you to ask which I should choose, a good wife or great riches,' said Mitya.

" 'Choose the good wife by all means,' the three peasants said promptly, 'A good wife is far better than all the riches upon earth.'

"So Mitya returned to the old man. 'Old Man,' he said, 'they tell me that I should ask for the good wife, and that I do.'

" 'Well chosen, young sir,' cried the old man. And he disappeared. In his place beside the youth there stood a beautiful maiden.

" 'Hail, Mitya, my bridegroom,' the maiden said. 'Let us go to the church and be wed. Then let us seek a place to set up our home.'

"Mitya and his good wife lived long, and sorrow and want never darkened their door. There was always plenty to eat and drink in Mitya's house—and all because of three kopecks and a cat."

The Wonderful Doll
of
Vasilla the Beautiful

"MY BASKET is half full, Sonia! How many have you?" Kyril cried to his sister. With old Nianya and several of her grandchildren, the brother and sister had spent the early morning hours picking mushrooms out in the forest. It had rained during the night, and the ground beneath the tall trees was dotted with the fat round heads of the mushrooms which Russians like so well to eat.

Each damp morning in autumn the peasants went forth from the great house to hunt for mushrooms on the mossy ground. They gathered them in their baskets and took them back to the kitchens, where they were salted in casks or strung upon strings to dry for use in the winter.

"I've not so many as you, but Nianya has three or four times as many as either of us," Sonia said, shaking her little basket.

"*Da, da,* my doves," said the old woman. "But my back is tired with bending and stooping. Let us sit down to rest on this log for a while. Then we can pick more."

Tall trees rose high above them. The pines looked black against the golden autumn colors of the other trees. Sonia peered behind her into the depths of the forest with its thicket of tree trunks.

"I should not like to go through the dark forest alone, Nianya," she said with a little shiver. "There must be foxes and wolves there, and one might so easily come upon a great bear."

"You would be safe if you had a wonderful doll to protect you, like the one which her mother gave to Vasilissa the Beautiful," the old woman said, wiping her red face with the corner of her apron. "Sit still here and rest a bit and I will tell you how Vasilissa went through the deep forest without harm or hurt.

"In the days of old there lived a certain merchant and his wife who had an only daughter called Vasilissa the Beautiful. When the child was about eight years old, her mother fell ill and, feeling herself about to die, she called her daughter to her bedside.

" 'Listen, my daughter,' she said to Vasilissa. 'Remember my dying words. Together with my mother's blessing upon you, I give you this doll. Take good care of it! Keep it always beside you, and never show it to anyone! If misfortune comes upon you, give the doll food to eat and ask its advice. It will protect you.' The mother then kissed her daughter, gave a long sigh, and died.

"Some years thereafter the merchant married again, and he chose as his wife a widow who had two daughters only a little older than Vasilissa. Through all the neighborhood the woman was known as a good housewife and a kind mother. But she turned out to be a very bad mother indeed for poor Vasilissa.

"Vasilissa was the most beautiful girl in all the country about, and so her stepmother and her daughters were jealous of her. They made her life miserable with their fault-finding and tormenting. They gave her hard work to do in the hope that it should make her scrawny and thin. They sent her out into the sun and wind so that her white skin might be tanned. Vasilissa never complained. Each day she became more and more lovely to look upon. As for the sisters, they grew ugly and thin from their malice and spite.

"The stepsisters could not understand it. How could it be that the girl could do such hard work and show no signs of weariness? I will tell you the secret, my little dears. It was the doll that helped Vasilissa. She could never have done such hard work alone. She kept the doll always near her. She saved for the doll bits of her supper each night, and the doll comforted her and helped her with her difficult tasks.

"So the years went by. The time came when the three sisters were of the right age to marry. All the gallants in the village wanted Vasilissa, and no one would look at her disagreeable stepsisters. Each time a suitor came to ask for Vasilissa, the angry stepmother would send him away, saying, 'No, the youngest shall not be wed before the oldest are married.' And when he had gone, poor Vasilissa would be scolded and beaten.

"Now the merchant one day set forth on a long journey, and while he was absent his wife moved into a house beside the deep forest. In the midst of this forest there was a glade. In the midst of the glade there was a hut. And in the hut there lived a dreadful old Baba Yaga who ate human beings as if they were chickens.

"Each day the merchant's wife sent Vasilissa into the wood, but each evening Vasilissa came home again safe and sound. The little doll warned her of the old Baba Yaga and kept her from going near the hut in the glade.

"One dark night in autumn the three sisters were working away in their house. One was knitting stockings, the second was making lace, and Vasilissa was spinning. The stepmother had put out all the lights in the house except one small candle by which the girls sat. This began to sputter and smoke, and one of the stepsisters took the pincers and trimmed it. In doing so, she purposely snuffed out the light.

" 'What shall we do now?" the stepsisters cried. 'There is no fire in the house to give us a light. Our tasks are not finished. We must run to the hut of the old Baba Yaga and ask for some fire.'

" 'The pins on my lace cushion give me enough light. I shall not go,' said the first of the stepsisters.

" 'My knitting needles shine brightly enough for me. I shall not go,' said the second stepsister. 'It is you that must go,' they cried to poor Vasilissa, and they pushed her out of the room. Vasilissa went into her little chamber. She set out the supper she had saved for the doll.

" 'There, Dolly. Feed! Help me in my need,' she said. 'I must go into the forest to the Baba Yaga for light, and she will surely eat me!'

" 'Have no fear, Vasilissa,' said the doll. 'Go where you are sent, but take me along with you and no harm will come.' So Vasilissa put the doll into her pocket. She made the Sign of the Cross and went into the deep forest.

"She walked and she walked through the dark wood. Suddenly there galloped past her a rider dressed all in white, riding on a white horse with trappings of white. And it began to grow light among the trees. Another rider galloped past. He was dressed in red, and he rode a red horse with trappings of red; and at the same moment the sun began to rise.

"On and on Vasilissa went. The whole day she walked, and towards evening she came to the glade where stood the house of the old Baba Yaga. Her heart was cold with fright when she saw that the fence around the witch's hut was made of bones and skulls. As she looked about in dismay, a third rider galloped up. He was dressed all in black, and he rode upon a black horse with trappings of black. And as he appeared, night fell on the forest.

"But it was not dark long. Fire shone from the eyes of the skulls on the fence and the whole glade was lighted. Just then there was a rush and a whir. The leaves rustled. The trees crackled. The Baba Yaga appeared, riding in a mortar, using a pestle as a whip, and sweeping away her traces with a great broom. She drove up to the gate. She sniffed the air thrice and then she cried out,

"'I smell a Russian! Who is here?'

"'It is I, Grandmother,' said Vasilissa, bowing before her. 'My stepsisters have sent me here to beg some fire from you.'

" 'Good!' said the Baba Yaga. 'I know your sisters well. I'll give you the fire, but you will have to work for me first.' ˙

"The gates opened wide. The Baba Yaga went in whistling, and Vasilissa followed her.

" 'Set out that which is in the oven,' the Baba Yaga roared. 'I want my supper!' Vasilissa lit a torch from the fire in one of the skulls, and she took out of the oven enough supper for ten persons. She brought *kvass*, mead, and wine from the cellar. The old woman ate and drank heartily. She left only a little cabbage soup and a crust of dry bread for Vasilissa. Before she climbed up on the stove for her night's sleep, she said to the girl:

" 'Tomorrow I go away. See to it that you sweep the yard, clean the hut, cook the dinner, wash the linen, and sort out a bushel of wheat. Be sure that you take out every black grain, or I'll eat you up.'

"When the old woman slept, Vasilissa set what remained from the supper before her little doll. 'There, Dolly. Feed! Help me in my need,' she cried, weeping bitterly. 'What a hard task I have! And if I do not do it, the Baba Yaga will eat me!'

" 'Fear not, Vasilissa,' the dolly replied. 'Sup, say your prayers, and then go to sleep. Morning is always wiser than evening.'

"Early, early next morning, Vasilissa awoke. The white rider galloped past, and it was day. The Baba Yaga came out into the yard and gave a shrill whistle. The mortar and pestle and broom all appeared, and the old woman rode off as the red rider flashed by and the sun rose.

" 'Which work shall I do first?' Vasilissa thought to herself. She looked about the hut. To her amazement the work was all done. The little doll was just sorting out the last grains of wheat. In the evening, as the black rider galloped past and the night came, the Baba Yaga returned.

" 'Is everything done?' she cried to the girl.

" 'Look and see for yourself, Grandmother,' Vasilissa replied. The Baba Yaga was vexed that there was nothing to complain of.

" 'All right,' she said, and then she called out, 'Hither, my trusty servants, come grind my wheat.' At her words there appeared three pairs of hands. They snatched up the wheat and carried it off.

" 'Tomorrow you shall do the work you have done to-day, and in addition sort one by one all the poppy seeds that you will find in the barn,' the Baba Yaga said to Vasilissa.

"The old woman settled herself upon the stove. While she slept and snored, Vasilissa took out her doll. She set out its supper, saying, 'There, Dolly. Feed! Help me in my

He rode a red horse with trappings of red.

need. What shall I do?' The doll answered as before: 'Sup, say your prayers, and go to sleep. Morning is always wiser than evening. All will be done as the Baba Yaga commands.'

"The old woman returned as night fell the next day. The work was all finished. 'Hither, my trusty servants,' she called. 'Come, press the oil out of the poppy seeds.' And three pairs of hands appeared and carried the poppy seeds away. Vasilissa stood by in silence as the old woman ate the supper she had prepared.

" 'Why do you not speak?' the Baba Yaga demanded. 'You act as though you were dumb.'

" 'Well, if I may, I'd like to ask you some questions,' Vasilissa said timidly.

" 'Go ahead,' said the Baba Yaga, 'only remember that not every question leads to good. If you know too much, you will soon grow old.'

" 'Well, Grandmother, when I was coming to you, I met a white rider. He was dressed in white, and he rode upon a white horse with trappings of white. Who is he?'

" 'That is my Bright Day,' said the Baba Yaga.

" 'And the red rider on the red horse with trappings of red. Who is he, Grandmother?'

" 'That is my Red Sun.'

" 'And the black rider on the black horse?'

" 'That is my Black Night, girl,' the old woman replied. 'Have you no more questions?' Vasilissa remembered the three strange pairs of hands, but she held her tongue.

" 'That will be enough, Grandmother,' she replied. 'You have said yourself that who knows too much will soon grow old.'

" 'It is well,' said the Baba Yaga, 'that you ask only about the things outside my courtyard, not the secrets within it. Now I shall ask a question of you. How is it that you could do the hard tasks that I have set for you?'

" 'It was the blessing of my mother that came to my aid,' said Vasilissa.

" 'Get thee gone!' cried the old woman. 'I want no blessed ones here!'

"She took Vasilissa into the courtyard and gave her one of the blazing skulls, which she stuck upon the end of a stick. 'Here is the fire for which your stepsisters sent you. Take it! Carry it home,' she said, starting the girl along on her way.

"Vasilissa ran through the forest as fast as she could. At the end of the second day she came to her home. She was about to throw the skull away, for she thought that surely by now they had fire in the house. But a voice came from the skull, saying, 'Do not throw me away! Carry me in and give me to your stepmother!'

"All the windows of the house were dark. Vasilissa entered, and for the first time in her life she was met with friendly words. Since she left the hut there had been neither fire nor light in it. Torches brought by the neighbors went out as soon as they entered the house. All was dark and cold.

"When Vasilissa came in with the skull, its eyes seemed to blaze brighter. Its flames shot forth in the direction of the stepmother and her two wicked daughters. Wherever they sought shelter, the flames followed them, and by morning they were all three burnt to a cinder. Vasilissa buried the skull in the ground and went forth to seek shelter until her father should come home.

"A poor woman took the girl into her house, and there she sat day after day, waiting and waiting. 'Little Mother,' she said at last to the woman, 'it is wearisome to sit idle. Go, buy me some flax and I will spin it for you.' The old woman brought her the flax, and the girl began to spin. The thread flew from her fingers, as even and fine as a hair on your head. So much did she spin that there was no more room in the hut. They sought for a loom upon which to weave the thread she had spun. But none could they discover fine enough for it.

"Vasilissa went to her doll for help and advice, and in one single night the doll had set up just the loom that was needed. When the thread was all woven, it made linen so fine that you could pass it through the eye of a needle. In the spring when the linen was whitened, Vasilissa gave it to the old woman and told her to sell it and keep the money for herself.

"The poor woman carried her linen to the palace and showed it to the Tsar. When he asked her its price, she gave it to him as a present, and in return she was showered with wonderful gifts. Then the Tsar had some shirts cut from the linen, but nowhere could he find a seamstress to sew them, the cloth was so fine. He sent again for the poor woman to come to the palace.

" 'You know how to spin and weave such fine linen, surely you must know how to make shirts of it,' the Tsar said to her.

" 'It was not I who spun or wove it, O Tsar,' the woman replied. 'It was a beautiful maiden who dwells in my cottage.'

" 'Well, let her sew the shirts,' the Tsar commanded. And the woman brought back the linen to Vasilissa. With the help of the doll, Vasilissa soon had a dozen shirts ready, and the old woman carried them again to the Tsar. Vasilissa washed her face and brushed her hair. She sat down near a window, and soon there came to her a messenger from the palace who said, 'My master, the Tsar, wishes to see for himself the maiden who made his beautiful shirts.'

"Vasilissa went with him to the royal palace. As soon as the Tsar saw her beauty, he fell in love with her. He seated her beside him on his great throne, and they were wed the same day.

"When the merchant came home from his journey, he was overjoyed at the happy fate of his daughter. Vasilissa the Beautiful brought her father to live in the palace with her, and she took into her service the poor woman who had sheltered her in her time of need. As for the doll, she carried it in her pocket till the very end of her life."

Marya Morevna

IN A certain kingdom in a certain state, there once lived a prince called Mikhail* and his three sisters, Vera, Anna, and Olga," said Nianya, beginning one of the *skazki* that Kyril and Sonia liked best. The old nurse was at work this afternoon in the linen room, making ready for the guests who would soon visit the great country house for the autumn hunting.

The children had come to find their Nianya and to beg for a fairy tale before dinner time. And, as always, Nianya was ready to call back for them the brave folk and the marvelous beasts of the olden days of the fairies.

"Now the father and mother of the Prince Mikhail

*Michael.

were dead, my little dears," Nianya continued. "Before he drew his last breath, the Tsar had spoken thus: 'Mikhail my son, give your sisters in marriage to the first suitors that come. Don't you go keeping them always at your side.'

"One day the Prince was walking with his three sisters in the green garden when suddenly black clouds covered the sky. A thunderstorm swept towards them. 'Let us hurry indoors,' cried the Prince, and they ran to the palace. Hardly had they set foot inside the hall when the storm broke. Lightning flashed. Thunder roared. The ceiling split open, and into the room there flew a fine falcon that straightway turned into a handsome young prince.

" 'Hail, Prince Mikhail,' cried the Falcon. 'I come as a suitor for the hand of your eldest sister, the Princess Vera.'

" 'If my sister so wishes, I will not say you nay,' Prince Mikhail replied. 'Marry her and God bless you!' The Princess consented. The next day they wed and the Falcon carried her off with him to his own kingdom.

"Hours came after hours. Days followed days. A whole year went by; and again Prince Mikhail and his two sisters walked about in their green garden. Again a thunderstorm drove them into their house. This time a great eagle flew down through the roof, and touching the floor, changed himself into a prince.

" 'Hail, Prince Mikhail,' said the Eagle. 'I come as a suitor for the hand of your second sister, the Princess Anna.' Well, Prince Mikhail gave his consent to their marriage also, and the Eagle Prince carried his bride away with him to his own kingdom.

Another year passed, and in like manner there came a Raven Prince who married Princess Olga and took her away, leaving poor Mikhail alone.

"Long were the days for the lonely Prince Mikhail. At last he decided to set forth to seek his three sisters and to pay them each one a visit. He rode and he rode. On his way he came to a plain upon which he saw a whole army of men lying dead beneath the blue sky. He wondered much at the sight, and he cried out in a loud voice, 'If there be living men among you, rise up and tell me who has slain this great host!'

" 'All have fallen by the sword of the Princess Marya Morevna,' a voice made reply. Prince Mikhail marveled at the tale of the beautiful Warrior Princess, and he turned his steps towards her white tent. She came forth to meet him, and he pleased her so well that she invited him to stay with her. Later they were married, and they returned to her kingdom to live in peace and contentment.

"But at last there came a day when the Warrior Princess decided to go forth to battle again. She left Mikhail be-

hind, saying, 'Go everywhere! See everything! But on no account look into yonder closet!'

"Well, of course, Marya Morevna had scarcely gone from the palace when Prince Mikhail rushed to the forbidden closet and opened the door. There he saw Kostchey the Sorcerer, fastened tight to the wall with twelve mighty chains.

" 'Have pity, O Mikhail Son-of-the-Tsar,' Kostchey said pleadingly. 'Have pity and give me a drink of cool water to wet my dry throat! Ten years have I hung here without food or drink.'

" 'To give a man drink is no very great sin,' Mikhail thought to himself. And he brought water to Kostchey. One bucket the Sorcerer drank! Two buckets! Then a third! With each draught, strength came to him, and as he took the last swallow, he gave a mighty lunge and broke all the twelve chains at once.

" 'My thanks to you, Prince,' he said to Mikhail, who was struck dumb with fear at what he had done. "But you have done yourself a bad turn. You will see your own ears sooner than you will lay eyes upon Marya Morevna again.' And he turned himself into a whirlwind and flew out of the window. He caught the Warrior Princess and carried her off with him to his far kingdom.

"Poor Prince Mikhail wept bitterly. He dressed himself and set forth in search of his bride. One day passed! Another day! And at dawn of the third day he saw a wonderful palace beside which was an oak tree. Upon the oak sat a fine falcon that flew down to earth upon his approach. The bird changed itself into a handsome young prince, and Mikhail saw that it was the bridegroom of his eldest sister, Vera.

"Well, Prince Mikhail stayed with the Falcon Prince and Vera in their palace for three days, and then he said he must set forth again to search for Marya Morevna.

" 'Hard will it be for you to find her,' answered the Falcon.

" 'But find her I will,' Mikhail replied. 'I will leave with you my silver spoon so that you may remember me. If it turns black, you will know that danger is threatening me. Then I pray you, my brother, come to my aid.' And he went along on his way.

"At dawn of the third day he came to the house of his sister Anna and her Eagle Prince. There, too, he rested three days, and on leaving he gave them his silver fork to remember him by. Likewise the Prince paid a visit to the Princess Olga and the Raven Prince, and with them he left his silver snuffbox.

"At last Mikhail arrived at the palace of Kostchey the Sorcerer, where he found his beloved Marya Morevna. She flung her arms round his neck and she burst into tears, so glad was she to see him again.

" 'Fly with me, dearest Marya,' Prince Mikhail begged. 'Kostchey is absent. Let us escape before he returns.' And they mounted Mikhail's horse and galloped away over the prairies.

"Now Kostchey was out hunting. Suddenly his horse

stumbled beneath him, and he scolded the steed, saying, 'Why dost thou stumbled, O Nag? Is danger approaching?'

" 'Prince Mikhail has carried off Marya Morevna,' the horse replied.

" 'Can we catch them?' asked Kostchey.

" 'We can sow wheat. We can wait till it ripens. We can reap it and thresh it and grind it into flour. We can make pies of the flour and eat them and even then be in time,' said the brave horse, and he began to fly like the wind.

"Kostchey soon caught up with the two runaways, and he brought them back to his palace. 'This time I forgive you,' he said to Prince Mikhail. 'Because you gave me water to drink and set me free, I will let you off.'

"A second time Prince Mikhail and Marya Morevna tried to escape. They galloped far, far away from the palace of the Sorcerer. And suddenly Kostchey, who was out on a hunt in the forest, felt his horse stumble beneath him.

" 'Prince Mikhail has fled again with Marya Morevna,' the horse said in reply to the Sorcerer's scolding.

" 'Can we catch him?' asked Kostchey.

" 'We can sow barley. We can wait till it ripens. We can thresh it and brew beer. We can drink the beer and take our sleep, and yet be in time,' the brave horse replied. And he galloped after the runaways with the speed of the north wind.

" 'A second time, I forgive you,' said Kostchey to Mikhail when he had overtaken him, 'but a third time, beware! I will cut you to pieces and throw you into the sea.'

"But Mikhail had no fear. A third time he placed Marya Morevna in front of him on his horse, and they galloped far, far away. And a third time Kostchey caught them. He cut the Prince into bits. He sealed the pieces up in a barrel which he covered with tar and threw into the sea.

"At the very same moment, in the palaces of his sisters, the silver fork, the silver spoon, and the silver snuffbox all turned black as night. The Eagle swooped down upon the sea and pulled the barrel from the blue waves. The Falcon flew to fetch the Water of Life, while the Raven brought thither the Water of Strength. They broke open the barrel and sprinkled the pieces with the two magic waters, and lo, there stood Prince Mikhail alive and well once again.

" 'What a time I have slept!' he said, stretching himself.

" 'You would have slept longer still, had it not been for us,' said the Eagle and the Falcon and the Raven princes. They wanted their brother-in-law to visit them in their palaces, but he refused, saying, 'I must go forth again to find my beloved Marya Morevna.'

"When he had come once more to the palace of Kostchey, Mikhail spoke thus in secret to the Warrior Princess: 'We must get for ourselves a fairy steed such as that upon which Kostchey rides abroad. Find out for me where he got his horse that flies like the wind, and I will go seek for one like it.'

" 'Beyond the thirtieth kingdom,' said Marya Morevna to Mikhail the very next morning, 'on the other side of the river of fire, there lives a Baba Yaga. She has a horse that gallops round the whole world in one single day. She has many other fine mares. It was from her that Kostchey got his steed that flies like the wind. He watched her mares for her for three days without losing one of them, and in return she gave him the steed upon which he always overtakes us.'

" 'How does Kostchey cross the river of fire?' Mikhail asked.

" 'By means of this kerchief,' said Marya Morevna. 'Wave it thrice to the right, and there arises a bridge so high the fire cannot touch it. Wave it three times to the left, and the bridge disappears.

"Marya gave Mikhail the magic kerchief, and he set out to find the old Baba Yaga and her wonderful mares. By the aid of the kerchief he crossed the river of fire safely, and he went on his way. He had had neither food to eat nor water to drink for a long time, when he came to the

277

nest of a strange bird in which he found several little ones.

" 'I'll eat these birds,' he said to himself. But the Mother Bird spoke to him, begging, 'Do not eat them, O Prince, and some time or other I will do you a good turn.' So he let the birds live and went on his way. Next he saw before him a beehive.

" 'Ha, some sweet honeycomb!' he cried. 'That will taste good!' But the Queen Bee flew to him and said: 'Do not eat our honey, Prince Mikhail. Leave it alone, and some day or other I will do you a good turn.' So he left it alone.

"Towards the end of his journey he came upon a Lioness with one little cub. 'I am so hungry,' he cried, 'that I could eat this baby lion.' But the Lioness begged him to let her cub live, promising that some day or other she would repay him.

"At last Prince Mikhail arrived at the house of the old Baba Yaga.

" 'Hail, Granny,' he said.

" 'Hail, Prince. Why have you come?'

" 'To earn a fine steed that flies like the wind.'

" 'Good!' said the old woman. 'Serve me for three days! Watch my mares without losing one, and I will give you a steed that flies so fast that even the north wind cannot catch it. But if you fail me, it will be the worse for you.'

"The Baba Yaga gave the Prince food and drink and sent him with the mares out to the meadows. No sooner were they in the fields than the horses threw up their heads and galloped away far out of sight.

"The Prince sat down on a stone and wept. Then he fell asleep. Towards nightfall the strange bird pecked at his arm, saying, 'Wake, Mikhail! Go home! The mares are all in their stables.' Meanwhile the Baba Yaga raged and stormed at her mares.

" 'Whatever did ye come home for?' she scolded.

" 'How could we help it?' the horses replied. 'Birds flew down upon us from all parts of the world. They all but pecked out our eyes!'

" 'Well, tomorrow you go galloping into the forests where the birds cannot see you,' the Baba Yaga commanded.

"In the morning Prince Mikhail went forth again with the mares. They cocked up their tails and galloped into the forest far, far out of sight. The Prince sat on a stone and wept. Then he fell asleep. At nightfall the Lioness came from the woods.

" 'Wake! Go home, Prince Mikhail!' she said. 'The mares are all in their stables.'

" 'Whatever did ye come home for?' the Baba Yaga scolded.

"'How could we help it?' the horses replied. 'Beasts of prey came running at us from all over the world. They would have torn us to pieces!'

"'Well, tomorrow you must hide yourselves in the blue sea,' the old woman cried.

"And so it happened. When Mikhail took the mares out on the third day, they tossed their heads and galloped off into the sea. Up to their necks in the water they stood, and they would not come out. Prince Mikhail wept. At last he went to sleep. At nightfall there came to him the Queen of the Honey Bees.

"'Wake, Prince Mikhail,' she said. 'The mares are all in their stables. But when you go home, do not let the Baba Yaga see you. Hide behind the mangers, and when she is asleep, take the sorriest colt and ride swiftly away.'

"When the Baba Yaga demanded why the mares had come home, they replied that all the bees that buzz under the sun had flown down and stung them until the blood came.

"At last when the old woman was sleeping and snoring, Mikhail rode away on the sorriest colt. At the river of fire he waved his kerchief thrice to the right and lo, there arose a high bridge. Once on the other side, the Prince waved his magic kerchief twice to the left, and the bridge became thin, oh, my doves, it was ever and ever so thin.

"Next morning the Baba Yaga missed her sorry colt. She rode off in pursuit upon her mare that flew like the wind. When she came to the river of fire, she saw the thin bridge and she tried to ride over it. But under her horse's galloping hoofs, the bridge broke in two parts, and the old woman plunged into the fiery river.

"Mikhail fattened his colt, and it became indeed the swiftest steed in the whole world. He sought Marya Morevna and put her up once more before him on his saddle. And they galloped far, far away. Now Kostchey was coming home from his day's hunting when his horse stumbled beneath him.

" 'Why dost thou stumble, O Nag?' Kostchey cried out.

" 'Prince Mikhail is carrying Marya Morevna away,' said the horse.

" 'Can we catch them?' asked Kostchey.

" 'Ah, that only God knows,' the horse said, tossing his head. 'Mikhail now has a horse that is swifter than I.'

" 'Well, we will try,' Kostchey declared. And they rode and they rode. Kostchey's horse went like the wind, but Mikhail's colt ran the faster, and Kostchey was forced to return alone to his palace. Mikhail took his bride to visit his sisters and their husbands, the Falcon, the Eagle, and the Raven.

" 'Welcome, brother,' they cried. 'We never expected to meet you again. But we can see that indeed it is not for nothing that you have given yourself so much trouble and pain. One might search the world over and not find such a beauty as your beloved Marya Morevna.' "

The
Greedy Priest

THERE goes the priest," said Nianya one day as she stood beside Kyril and Sonia at their playroom window. She was looking down at the driveway along which was walking the priest from the white church in the village. "He has been bothering the master again with his complaints, or asking for money like the very worst beggar that comes to town upon feast days," she complained.

Nianya did not like this priest. She was a pious woman. Each morning and each night she was careful to say her prayers before the holy pictures, the icons, which she had hung in the corner of her chamber. She never entered a room in the great house without turning to its icon corner and crossing herself, and she always went to the church for its feasts and its services. She believed in the saints and kept their days well.

But like the rest of the peasants, Nianya mistrusted this particular priest. He was all right for weddings and funerals and for saying Mass. But as a man—well, she often told the children there was no one more greedy in all holy Russia.

"*Da*, my little pigeons," she said to Kyril and Sonia as the priest walked toward the gates. "There goes a greedy man. He cheats the poor peasants and he takes their last kopecks. Did he not refuse to marry poor Yasha because he had not quite enough kopecks saved up to pay him his fee! He is as greedy as the priest who tried to cure the sick girl, as though he were a saint."

"What is that tale, Nianya?" Kyril asked curiously.

"It goes this way," said the woman. "Once there lived a priest. He was poor—oh, dreadfully poor. Was it because his parish was small, or was there some other reason? I do not know. But the truth is he was always praying to God and Saint Nicholas that his fortune should be bettered and that he should in some way get money.

"But God did not send him luck. He grew poorer and poorer, and at last he determined to get out and seek his fortune in another state. He locked the church door and left his little house empty. He went on and on, wherever his eyes led him.

"He walked and he walked, and at last one day he met two travelers seated on the roadside. They were two men dressed just like himself, with knapsacks slung on their backs. It was plain that they had sat down for a moment to rest after a long, wearisome journey. One was a young man with a little beard, and the other was older. You see, they were really two of the good saints, and one was the merciful Saint Nicholas himself.

" 'Where are you going, my dear brothers?' said the priest. 'I see that you are wayfarers just as I am.'

" 'Ah, brother,' they replied, 'we are men who see many things that are hidden from others. We are doctors who go about making marvelous cures.'

" 'Excellent!' said the priest. 'Take me along with you.'

" 'Come, then,' they replied. 'Only mark you, we share everything that we get equally between the three of us.'

" 'Of course,' the priest consented. 'How else should it be? Of course we shall share equally.'

"So all three walked on together. On and on they went, and when they grew tired they went into a hut to rest for the night. Now Saint Nicholas and his brother saint had only one small loaf of bread between them. They laid it carefully away on the shelf under the icons so as to have it ready for breakfast early next morning.

"Well, the priest arose at the sunrise. His stomach was empty. He spied the small loaf of bread, and he slyly took it and ate it all by himself. Later, when Saint Nicholas awoke, he saw at once that his small loaf of bread was not where he had left it.

" 'Who has taken my small loaf of bread?' Saint Nicholas asked.

" 'How should I know?' said the dishonest priest. 'Indeed, I have not eaten it!'

"The saints said no more. The three went along on their way, walking and walking. At last they drew near a city.

" 'Here there is a rich *boyar* who has a sick daughter,' Saint Nicholas said to his companions. 'No one can cure her. Let us go and give her our aid.' So they came to the house of the rich nobleman. They knocked at the window, and Saint Nicholas called out: 'Let us in, O Boyar! We have come to cure your daughter!' So they were let in, and the nobleman gave them permission to try to make his daughter well once again.

"Saint Nicholas brought her to the steam bathhouse out in the courtyard. He built a great fire in the stove and heated the water. Then he took a sharp knife and cut the girl into pieces. She could not have felt it at all, for she did not cry out. The good saint washed the pieces in three different waters and he put them together again, just as before. He sprinkled them once, and her body became whole. He sprinkled them twice, and she began to move about. A third time he sprinkled her, and she arose, well again. They brought her to her father, and she rushed to him, crying:

" 'O Little Father, I am well! I am quite well again!'

"So the nobleman ordered a great feast for the three doctors. He set rich meats and good drinks before them. Saint Nicholas and his brother saint tasted the food and were easily satisfied. But the greedy priest ate and ate until he was so full that he could scarcely rise from the table. Then the nobleman opened his money chests and said, 'Take all the roubles you wish—all that you can carry.'

"Now Saint Nicholas took a small handful, and the other saint did likewise. But the greedy priest began to store away gold all over his person. Into his pockets, into his knapsack, under his belt, and in his top boots—into each nook and corner he crammed fistfuls of gold.

"Then the three started out again on their journey. On and on they went, and at last they came to a deep river. The two saints walked over the waters ever so easily. But the greedy priest with the heavy gold stored all about him began to sink at once. He felt he was drowning, and he called out for help from the two saints on the opposite bank of the stream.

"'Throw the money into the river!' they shouted. Throw it away or you will drown!'

" 'No, I will not throw the money away, and I will not drown,' the greedy priest cried. And after all, he managed somehow or other to get across the deep river with all the money upon him.

"Well, all three sat down on the opposite bank. Saint Nicholas then said, 'Now is the time for us to divide up the money into our equal shares.' And he and the other saint poured out their gold upon the ground.

"But the greedy priest held tight to his pockets and his

knapsack. 'This is my money,' he cried. 'Why did you two not bring more away with you? I nearly drowned because of this money which you wanted me to throw away into the river.'

" 'Is not your promise worth more than money?' Saint Nicholas said.

"Well, at that the priest felt ashamed. He poured out his roubles upon those of the two saints. Saint Nicholas began to divide them, and the greedy priest was surprised to see him making four piles.

" 'We are but three,' he said to the saint. 'For whom is the fourth pile?'

" 'The fourth pile is for the greedy one who ate our small loaf of bread,' said good Saint Nicholas.

" 'Listen, brother! Oh, listen! it was I,' cried the priest. 'I ate the loaf, so it is I who shall then have two portions of the money.'

" 'Take my part as well,' said good Saint Nicholas, in disgust.

" 'And mine, too,' said the other saint! Now you have so much, go along home. We shall travel alone.'

"The greedy priest took the money and turned his face homeward. But as he walked he began to think: 'Why should I go home? Why should I not cure people as the two travelers do? I should get a great deal more money.

I have seen how it is done. I can do it quite as well as they.'

"So the foolish priest went on and on until he came to a city where he learned of a rich merchant whose daughter was ill. No one could cure her, and the poor father was in despair. The foolish priest knocked on his window and made the rich merchant believe that he was a doctor. He asked for a sharp knife, and he led the poor girl into the steam bathhouse out in the courtyard. He made a fire in the stove and heated the water as he had seen Saint Nicholas do. Then he began cutting the girl up into pieces. But the girl began shrieking. She called and she cried.

" 'Don't cry, I say, don't cry,' said the priest anxiously. 'You will soon be well.' And he cut her to bits. Then he began washing the pieces and trying to put them together again. He worked and he worked, and at last somehow or other he managed to lay the pieces as they should be! Then he sprinkled them once. He sprinkled them twice. He sprinkled them three times, but yet nothing came of it.

" 'Oh dear, I am lost! Oh dear, they will hang me! oh dear, they will send me to far-off Siberia!' he wailed to himself. And he began praying to God and to good Saint Nicholas that they should send him the two doctors with whom he had traveled.

"In his distress the priest looked out of the window, and

he cried out with joy when he saw the two doctors coming straight to the bathhouse. The young man with a beard was there, and also the little old one. Oh, but he was glad to see them, my doves! He flopped down on his knees and kissed their dusty boots.

"'O Little Fathers,' he cried, 'treat me like a kinsman! Come to my aid! I have tried to make a cure just as you did, but no good has come of it!'

"Now, of course, you remember that the two travelers were none other than Saint Nicholas the Miracle-Worker and a fellow-saint.

"'You have undertaken too much, O Greedy Priest,' the saints said, smiling at the poor fellow's distress. Then Saint Nicholas took the pieces of the poor girl and washed them. He put them together and sprinkled them with water. Lo, her body became whole! He sprinkled them a second time, and she began to move. A third time he sprinkled them, and the girl arose, alive and well. The priest made the Sign of the Cross over her head. 'Oh, how glad I am!' he cried. 'How glad I am, I can't tell you!'

"'Now take her to her father,' Saint Nicholas said. 'But don't you go about trying to cure the sick as we do. For we will not come again, and another time you will be lost.' Then the two saints left the courtyard, and the greedy priest never saw them again.

"The greedy priest brought the girl to her father and said: 'Behold! She is cured.' And the daughter declared that she was well. So the merchant set out a feast for the greedy priest. He tried to persuade him to remain in his household in case his daughter should fall ill once again. But the priest shook his head, crying:

" 'Oh no! Oh no! I could not remain!' The merchant gave him much money, a horse, and a cart. And the priest drove straight home, vowing before God that he would never—no, never—try to cure a sick person again."

The Enchanted Lime Tree

 OR days the great country house had been filled with guests for the autumn hunting. Each morning early the hunting party rode forth under the blue sky, galloping across the wide prairies, around the green marshes and through the thick forests with their bright leaves of flame color and gold. The hunters looked fine in their long hunting coats, their high boots, and their red and black Cossack caps.

Kyril and Sonia rode along with them on their ponies for some of the shorter hunts. The children always enjoyed the excitement of the fall hunting season. They liked the sound of the horns of the huntsmen and the baying of the hounds as they leapt away in pursuit of a hare or a fox.

Sonia usually rode beside the head huntsman, and only yesterday he had given her the skin of a fox which he had killed, to make herself a tippet.

The talk about the samovar at tea each day was all about hunting and the animals that each man had killed. Kyril's father had brought out his wolf heads and his bear skins to show to his guests. He had shot the beasts in the cold winter time, when the snow covers the ground and when the tracks of the animals are more easily seen.

Upstairs in the playroom on this afternoon the talk was also of hunting. Kyril had draped a bear skin over his shoulders and was crouched down in a corner beside the tall stove. Sonia was trying to drive him out of his den. Nianya was holding her plump sides with laughter at the children's antics. Suddenly the boy stood up on his feet. He waved the bear's forepaws at his little sister. Then he rushed at her and threw the hairy arms round her in a mighty squeeze. Sonia squealed as she struggled out of his grasp and rushed to hide behind Nianya.

"Gently, now Kyril, dear," the old nurse called out. "You play far too roughly. That's enough for today."

"Why is it, Nianyuska, that bears' paws are so much like the hands and feet of a man?" Kyril asked as he threw off the heavy bearskin and laid it again in its place on the floor.

"Listen and I will tell you a story about that which I heard from the old folks when I was a child," Nianya said to the boy. "You see, once, long before our grandfathers and great grandfathers lived, bears were people like you and me and other good Christians. Now in those days there was, in a certain village, a peasant named Bobyl who lived with his wife in a small wretched hut. He was so poor that he had not even a horse, and he could not remember the time when a cow stood in his stable.

"Well, winter came and it was cold—oh, so cold! There was no fire in the stove and no wood with which to make one. So Bobyl shouldered his axe and went forth into the forest.

"He walked and he walked, and at last he came to a certain place where there stood a tall Lime Tree. Bobyl struck it with his axe, thinking to cut it down and chop it up into sticks. But to his surprise a voice came from the trunk of the tree.

" 'Hold, Peasant,' it said. 'Do not cut me down! Spare me, and whatever you wish, that I shall do for you.'

" 'Ha, Little Mother Lime Tree!' Bobyl cried. 'How splendid that will be! Make me richer than all the other peasants in our village! As I am now, I have neither horse nor cow, and my house is a wretched little hovel indeed.'

" 'Go home, Bobyl,' said the Lime Tree. 'All will be

awaiting you.' And the peasant hurried back to the village to find his hut changed into a new house with a fine wood fence around it. His barn was filled with good grain, and as for his horses, why, when he looked at them in his stable he felt just like flying, he was so happy. Only his wife was as ugly as before. He scowled as he looked at her. What was to be done? She did not fit in at all with his new splendor. So he decided to go once more to visit the Lime Tree.

"Bobyl took his axe over his shoulder, and he set out for the forest. When he came to the Lime Tree, he struck the trunk a mighty blow.

" 'What do you want?' asked the Lime Tree.

" 'Ah, Little Mother Lime Tree!' cried Bobyl. 'One wife is not like another. Now mine is good for nothing. She is ugly and old. Do me this favor! Change her into a pretty young wife!'

" 'Go home, Bobyl. Your pretty young wife awaits you,' said the voice from the Lime Tree. When the peasant reached his hut, there stood in the doorway a beautiful young woman, with skin like red blood and white milk. And besides this, his storeroom was filled to the roof with all sorts of good things.

"Well, Bobyl lived happily with his pretty young wife and his new riches for many years. But one day the thought came to him: 'It is nice to be rich, but still I am not free.

I must always do as the village elders decree. Would it not be better if I should become a village elder myself?' He talked the matter over with his wife, and then he set forth to visit the Little Mother Lime Tree once more. He arrived in the forest and struck the trunk of the Lime Tree a hearty blow with his axe.

" 'What do you wish, Little Peasant?' the Lime Tree demanded.

" 'Well, Mother Lime Tree,' said Bobyl, 'I will tell you. Though I am now well-to-do, I am not free. I must do as I am told by the elders of the village. Would I not be better off if I were also an elder?'

" 'Go home, Bobyl,' said the Lime Tree. 'It shall be as you wish.'

"Bobyl had not yet had time to take off his sheepskin coat, when there came to his door a message from the village council, to say that he, Bobyl, the peasant, had been elected an elder.

"But new things soon become old, my doves, and so it was with Bobyl. The newness of his position as village elder quickly wore off and became an old story. 'To be sure, I am a village elder,' Bobyl said to his wife. 'But still the noble lord is above me. Would it not be nice if I, too, might be a lord?'

"Again Bobyl went into the forest, and again he struck

the trunk of the Lime Tree a ringing blow with his axe.

" 'What do you wish now?' the Lime Tree asked him.

" 'First, my thanks to you, dear Little Mother Lime Tree, for all you have given me,' Bobyl said politely. 'But though I am well off and am an elder in the village, still I have to bow to the noble lord. How would it be if, instead of doffing my cap and bending the knee before the nobles, I were a noble myself?'

" 'Go home, Bobyl,' said the Lime Tree. 'Do not worry; it shall be done.' And upon his arrival at his own house Bobyl was met by the governor of the province, who handed him a paper signed by the Tsar. 'Bobyl is from henceforth a noble lord,' was written upon it. Well, it was good indeed to be a noble lord, thought Bobyl. But there were many greater than he. He thought much about this. He discussed it with his wife, and again he went to the forest.

" 'What do you wish, Little Peasant?' the Lime Tree asked Bobyl.

" 'Well, I thank you for all you have done for me,' said the man, 'but there are many nobles of greater degree than myself. Can you not make me a high official?'

" 'Go home, Bobyl,' said the Lime Tree. 'It shall be done.'

"And it was done, my dears! Bobyl received another

paper, signed by the Tsar, raising his rank and bringing him new importance. You would have thought that he would now be content, but he said to himself: 'Alas, I am under the rule of the governor of the province. It would be far better if I myself might be made governor.'

" 'What is it you need now?' the Lime Tree inquired when Bobyl struck it again.

" 'Little Mother Lime Tree,' he said, 'indeed I am not ungrateful, but I should like it better if I might become governor of the whole province, with a great estate to be handed down to my son and to his son after him.'

" 'Go home, Bobyl,' said the Lime Tree. 'This will not be easy, but have no fear, I will manage it.'

"Well, Bobyl became governor of the whole province, and he lived on an estate even finer than ours. He grew so used to his life in high places that he almost forgot that he had been born a poor peasant. Yet even now the foolish Bobyl was not satisfied.

" 'It is well to be governor and to own a splendid estate,' he said to his wife, 'but I am always under the power of the Tsar. How would it be if I were made Tsar myself?' His wife was frightened at his words. But she, too, thought how fine it would be to become the Tsarina and to sit on the throne. And so she did not prevent him from going out to the forest to visit the Lime Tree.

And as the lime tree ceased speaking,
Bobyl turned into a bear!

"'What can be the matter, now?' the Lime Tree demanded as Bobyl's axe struck her trunk once again.

"'Ah, Little Mother Lime Tree!' said Bobyl. 'All is well. I am indeed grateful for your kindness. To be sure, I am governor, but still I am not free. I am under the Tsar. How would it be if I asked you to make me Tsar, myself?'

"'Foolish man!' said the Lime Tree. 'Take care! You ask too much. Think of what you were and of what you are now! Think of Bobyl, the poor peasant, without a horse or cow! Then think of Bobyl, the governor, with his fine estate and his stables filled with horses and cattle! Remember foolish man, our Tsar is chosen by God.' And the enchanted Lime Tree tried to keep foolish Bobyl from demanding the impossible.

"But the man would not give in. 'I wish to be Tsar! I command you to make me Tsar, O Lime Tree!' he cried, and he struck the tree trunk a great blow with his axe.

"'It cannot be done! It will not be done! I warned you, Bobyl! Now you shall lose everything!'

"And as the Lime Tree ceased speaking, Bobyl turned into a bear! He waddled off through the forest and was met by his wife, whom the Lime Tree had changed into a she-bear. Gone were their house and their horses, their cattle and other riches! And from that day to this, bears like Bobyl have lived in the forests. The only thing to remind them of the days when they were like other Christians are their forepaws and hindpaws which so much resemble the hands and feet of a man."

"Is that a true story, Nianya?" Kyril demanded.

"Of course not, my dove," the old nurse replied. "But what does that matter? You must not ask the impossible. Be content with a little or you may lose all, like foolish Bobyl."